A NEW C

AND AN ANCIENT EVIL

JANE ADDAMS

A New Conscience and an Ancient Evil

INTRODUCTION BY
KATHERINE JOSLIN

University of Illinois Press
URBANA AND CHICAGO

Introduction © 2002 by Katherine Joslin
All rights reserved
Manufactured in the United States of America
1 2 3 4 5 C P 5 4 3 2 1
∞ This book is printed on acid-free paper.

Library of Congress Cataloging-in-Publication Data
Addams, Jane, 1860–1935.
A new conscience and an ancient evil / Jane Addams.
p.   cm.
Includes bibliographical references and index.
ISBN 0-252-02784-1 (cloth : alk. paper)
ISBN 0-252-07092-5 (paper : alk. paper)
1. Prostitution. 2. Prostitution—Illinois—Chicago.
I. Title.
HQ144.A7   2002
306.74—dc21   2002000262

To the Juvenile Protective Association of Chicago,
whose superintendent and field officers have collected
much of the material for this book, and whose
president, Mrs. Joseph T. Bowen, has so ably and
sympathetically collaborated in its writing.

Contents

Introduction   *ix*
  Katherine Joslin

Preface   *1*

1. As Inferred from an Analogy   *3*

2. As Indicated by Recent Legal Enactments   *9*

3. As Indicated by the Amelioration of
   Economic Conditions   *26*

4. As Indicated by the Moral Education and Legal
   Protection of Children   *45*

5. As Indicated by Philanthropic Rescue
   and Prevention   *64*

6. As Indicated by Increased Social Control   *82*

Index   *101*

Introduction:
Slum Angels

KATHERINE JOSLIN

✍ "There comes a time in nearly every girl's life when her cry is to go to the city," Florence Mabel Dedrick, a missionary at the Moody Church in Chicago, declared.[1] As Melville's Ishmael and his generation of young men on the East Coast headed for the sea in the nineteenth century, midwestern girls headed for Chicago. Dedrick's essay "Our Sister of the Street," which aroused the reading public, appeared in a sensational exposé entitled *Fighting the Traffic in Young Girls; or, The War on the White Slave Trade.* The illustration on the book's cover features a white woman locked behind bars, a pale but shapely young victim who has a slim waist, bare shoulders, and long, wavy hair. Her eyes are turned hopefully upward to heaven, and a ghostly male figure lurks in the shadows. The book contains a series of essays on the sex trade in Chicago, contributions written by such public figures as Edwin W. Sims, a U.S. district attorney, and Clifford G. Roe, a state's attorney.

Jane Addams, from her upstairs window at Hull-House, could look down onto Halsted Street and witness the cultural change taking place in America. She could catch glimpses of newly arrived rural "girls" whom she would imaginatively reconstruct as characters in many books about the texture of cities at the turn of the nineteenth century. "As these overworked girls stream along the street," she noted, "the rest of us see only the self-conscious walk, the giggling speech, the preposterous clothing, and yet through the huge hat, with its wilderness of bedraggled feathers, the girl announces to the world that she is here."[2]

Perhaps no figure intrigued the American middle-class reading public more than the lithe young woman under the bedraggled feathers. Any writer eager for a large audience needed a seemingly tragic plot that threatened defenseless city girls and yet in the end secured their rescue by allowing them to remain angels, albeit of the slums. Princess Alice of Windsor, having read *Twenty Years at Hull-House,* urged Jane Addams to tell the story of sexually vulnerable young urban women: "Their youth and inexperience, linked with their slender resources and lack of knowledge of the language, expose them to the unforeseen and grave dangers in a strange land, where many watch them for evil and few have any regard for their good."[3] The suggestion would have provided an able blurb for a book Addams would complete in the winter of 1912: *A New Conscience and an Ancient Evil.*

Getting beyond the histrionics of white slavery (an international conspiracy to exploit young women and girls) to tell prosaic stories about female experience in the city was nearly impossible for writers. Addams's study of prostitution struggles to portray poor women in Chicago as mobile, intelligent, experimental, pugnacious, and imaginative, but it fails to get beyond the image of the white slave. Addams wrote for an audience obsessed with the vulnerability of untended girls from Europe or rural America, imperiled by the seductions of urban life. In the popular imagination, young women adrift in the city were unsuspecting victims of sexual predators. The public preferred a tale of seduction and betrayal to a more realistic depiction of young women forging neighborhood communities, organizing labor unions, claiming their places in the city, and even shaping the manners and mores of middle-class America. Ostensibly, investigations of the sex trade served as warnings intended to save young women from crime, but in reality they limited movement into the city and curbed freedom, professional and educational as well as sexual, once the women got there.

Sexual slavery functioned then, as it sometimes does now, as an urban myth used to frighten adventurous women whose "cry is to go to the city." Florence Dedrick understood that cry, because she, too, preferred city life. Addams had also come to Chicago at the age of twenty-nine with Ellen Gates Starr. The two women, both from small towns, established a social settlement in 1889 on Halsted Street, a synergetic immigrant neighborhood. Publicly, they gave building a profession as their reason for coming to the city. Hull-House was to be a model for social work, a decidedly female project in America.

Chicago offered professional women freedom from the demands of family life and entrée into the cultural and social life of the city. Dedrick was quick to separate her own activities and those of other professional women from the activities of poor and working-class women. A woman's movement into the city "may be necessary through force of circumstances, or to develop herself along the line of her cherished ambition, or a thirst for knowledge," Dedrick argues, certain her reasons for coming to Chicago involved missionary calling, professional ambition, and a desire to know about the wider world. Although women at Hull-House had come to Chicago for those reasons as well, Dedrick thought that the majority of rural and immigrant women had arrived for motives she viewed as less justifiable than her own. "If it is to satisfy the desire for mere personal happiness and enjoyment and craving for excitement, I say, 'Beware!' for here it is many slip and are lost," she cautioned.[4] Any woman desiring happiness, enjoyment, or excitement was under suspicion, and any who succumbed to sexual cravings put herself beyond social respectability and religious salvation.

It is difficult in the twenty-first century to imagine the distance between licit and illicit sex in the early twentieth century, the borderland Addams sought to depict in her book. Sexuality, then as now, was tied to gender but perhaps more so to social class and race. Chicago's population tripled between 1880 and 1900, bringing thousands of poor women—European immigrants, rural Americans, and African Americans from the South—to the city. Close quarters in tenements moved men and women into the streets and into public places such as dance halls, ice cream parlors, amusement parks, and nickelodeon theaters, where they intermingled familiarly. Chaperones rarely featured in urban life as they did in small-town America and middle-class society, and gossip often lost its power amid the many languages and cultures of an urban neighborhood.

Crime commissions and social reformers, reacting emotionally to images of young women, loose and unchaperoned, labeled a wide variety of activities as "prostitution." Kathy Peiss has discovered in the actual records of the time that many young women considered dancing, flirting, touching, kissing, and trading ribald jokes with working men as part of the manners and mores of their social class. They also exchanged sex for what Peiss calls "treats," things they could not afford to buy with earnings from factory work, domestic service, or even sales and clerical jobs. As George Kneeland found in his contemporary research into prostitution, women (often known as "charity girls") generally refused direct payment for sexual favors and sought instead presents, attention, and pleasure from encounters with men.[5]

Historians have noted a central irony concerning the vice commissions of the turn of the last century. Moral panic over prostitution and sexual slavery in the United States came at a time when prostitution may have been waning because availability of birth control devices allowed freer sexual behavior. A perception that there was freer sexuality among middle-class women may explain the exaggerated attention given to "white slaves."

The issue of sexual slavery in the United States grew out of a British movement against regulating prostitution, an issue led by Addams's friend William Stead and Josephine Butler, another crusader, who argued that to regulate prostitution was to sanction it. Stead, a zealot in the crusade against white slavery in Great Britain, had arranged to "buy" thirteen-year-old Eliza Armstrong from her parents for 5 pounds in order to prove that sexual slavery was indeed a national issue. He then used his success in the Armstrong incident to launch a series of articles— "The Maiden Tribute of Modern Babylon"—in the *Pall Mall Gazette* in 1885. Stead was also the author of *If Christ Came to Chicago!* (1894), an exposé of the sins of that city.

International conferences on sexual slavery—in Geneva in 1877, Genoa in 1880, and Paris in 1902—led to the International Agreement for the Suppression of the White Slave Traffic, which twelve nations ratified in 1904. The United States responded with the Mann Act in 1910, prohibiting the movement of women across state lines for purposes of sexual activity. More than a thousand people were prosecuted under the act from 1910 to 1918, most of them for activities that had nothing to do with white slavery. Judith Walkowitz notes that public outrage over sexual slavery dislodged feminists from power in England, ironically handing the problem of prostitution over to male professionals, conservative churchmen, and advocates of social purity.[6] Another, perhaps unintended, consequence of the campaign against white slavery was that the social purity movement advocated burning and condemning some works of literature, especially novels by Honoré de Balzac,

Émile Zola, and François Rabelais in Europe. Sister movements in the United States scrutinized the work of Theodore Dreiser, particularly his novels based on his sisters' experiences in Chicago.[7] Although contemporaries and scholars have found evidence of schemes to sexually enslave girls, the moral panic appears to have been a gross exaggeration. Teresa Billington-Grieg, for example, called into question the sensational accounts of the period in "The Truth about Sexual Slavery" (1913)—the truth being that she could find no official proof that "organized trapping" was occurring. The following year in Massachusetts a crime commission reported that stories of white slavery appeared to be based on hearsay and fiction: "Several of the stories were easily recognized versions of incidents in certain books or plays." The genre established a stylized plot that worked its way into fiction as well as into supposed reports of fact. For all the fear of danger to and from poor immigrant women, Ruth Rosen and Barbara Meil Hobson have found that prostitutes in Boston, New York, and Philadelphia tended to come from the upper lower class. They were American-born daughters of immigrant artisans and farmers and often held other jobs and then later married.[8]

That is not to suggest that women were not coerced into sex for money. Coercion, however, often took the form of economic necessity, the "beast" Emma Goldman metaphorically identified as "exploitation, of course; the merciless Moloch of capitalism that fattens on underpaid labor, thus driving thousands of women and girls into prostitution."[9] Goldman, agreeing with Charlotte Perkins Gilman's sociological study *Women and Economics* (1899), voiced the radical view that the only difference between marriage and prostitution was "merely a question of degree whether [a woman] sells herself to one man, in or out of marriage, or to many men." Economic conditions prohibited single women from living on their own; factory workers or clerks earned only $8 to $10 per week in 1910, hardly enough to pay for room and board and certainly not enough to pay for clothing or amusement. Addams considered women in the neighborhood around Hull-House and was concerned that they might fall prey to bartering their sexuality, which for her was worse than trading sex for the financial security of middle-class marriage. "Their unspoiled human nature, not yet immune to the poisons of city life, when thrust into the midst of that unrelieved drudgery which lies at the foundation of all complex luxury," Addams warned, "often results in the most fatal reactions" (p. 73).

Ruth Rosen sees a good deal of pragmatism in the face of economic pressure, concluding that prostitution was "a dangerous and degrading occupation that, given the limited and unattractive alternatives . . . enabled thousands of women to escape even worse danger and deprivation."[10] The sex trade, in fact, involved young women who wandered in and out of the business during their early lives and left the trade as raises in pay for other labor allowed. David Graham Phillips's two-volume novel *Susan Lenox: Her Fall and Rise* (1917) plots such an upward course for his fallen heroine in a narrative that may have come close to the experiences of many American women. In *Sister Carrie* (1900), Dreiser recounts a version of his sister Emma's experiences, but the dénouement allows Carrie to become wealthy if not content. The purity leagues gave him such grief about the ambivalent ending that his second novel, *Jennie Gerhardt* (1911), was sharply bowdlerized before Harper's would publish it. The novel followed the familiar contours of the white slavery narrative.

The report of the Vice Commission of Chicago typified the official portrait of female sexual vulnerability: "Huddled away among coarse and vulgar male companions, lonely, underfed and hungry—hungry not only for food, but for a decent shelter, for a home, for friends, for a sympathetic touch or word; tired from a hard day's toil even to the point of recklessness—starving for honest pleasures and amusements—and with what does she meet?"[11] Huddled, hungry, filthy, outside the shelter of a sympathetic sisterhood, and tainted by the indecencies of male companionship, poor women were seen as easy prey for white slavery. Although the word *white* explicitly distinguished the trade from black slavery, it tacitly supported racism in American culture by focusing attention on the sexual enslavement of European-American women, even though traffic in women of color, especially Asian women sold in California, was more verifiable.[12]

The issue generated thousands of Vice Commission reports, vigilance committee exposés, newspaper accounts, magazine warnings, and books that featured versions of the white slavery narrative, a sentimental genre akin to nineteenth-century novels of seduction and rescue. The twenty-four-hour, seven-day-a-week CNN phenomenon at the turn into the twenty-first century mirrors the print-media's concentration on white slavery in the years leading up to World War I. Once the nation began its slide into the war in Europe, however, readers abandoned the issue. A sex slave in "actual" accounts and fictive portrayals was young, beautiful, passive, inarticulate, and usually white—an "angel of the slums." Fact and fiction, as the crime commission in Massachusetts noticed, borrowed from each other, and it was difficult to know, either then or now, what the women may have experienced.

Narratives of white slavery, like those of the Juvenile Protective Association report Jane Addams used for her examples, follow a fairly regular pattern. A poor woman, always young and beautiful and usually white, leaves the country for the city or Europe for America. She finds herself tricked by wily slave traders—dark, suspicious types, often Jews or Italians, who lie in wait at train stations, hotels, dance halls, ice cream parlors, and movie houses or linger outside sweatshops and department stores. The swarthy men promise marriage or offer help with lodging. They might drug the heroine with chloroform or spiked drinks and haul her off to a brothel, where they force her to surrender her street clothes for filmy, lacy, flashy garments and lock her up. Her debasement and isolation heighten a plot meant to arouse readers, who get to peek at a life of sexual excess and the rape of innocence from comfortable, middle-class armchairs.

The white slavery narrative offered a reductive, stylized version of female sexual experience in response to what Jeffrey Weeks terms a "moral panic" over the relocation of poor women to the city.[13] As Peter Stallybrass and Allon White theorize, the cultural elite may seek to eliminate those who are socially lower as a measure of prestige and status. Yet they may also, ironically, embrace what they consider to be low as a "primary eroticized constituent of [their] own fantasy life." The dynamic results in a seeming paradox: "What is *socially* peripheral is so frequently *symbolically* central."[14]

Socially marginal poor women, alone in the city and often immigrants or the daughters of immigrants, came to symbolize the central matters surrounding women and social change in America. Current issues coalesced around them, including the movement of women away from the domestic sphere, female sexuality, divorce, birth control, venereal disease, female education, and even suffrage. Equally of concern were trepidation over the rapid influx of immigrants to American cities, suspicion of differing racial and ethnic groups, fear of miscegenation and the taint of foreign blood, lamentation over the loss of rural agrarian culture, and anxiety over the strength of urban industrial capitalism.[15] Poor women were pressed by economic necessity, reared outside genteel society, and often rebellious against immigrant customs. Moreover, they threatened the American middle class, which feared they might ignore their social codes, manners, and mores.

The pressure "on young woman workers," Addams concludes, might cause social and economic rebellion. "The long hours, the lack of comforts, the low pay, the absence of recreation, the sense of 'good times' all about her which she cannot share, the conviction that she is rapidly losing health and charm," Addams warns middle-class readers, "rouse the molten forces within her" (p. 36). The molten forces suggest a power that might lead to labor unions; political demonstrations; and insistence on radical change in family life, domesticity, sexuality, and labor as well as the merging and blending of ethic and racial groups in the city. Addams approaches a revolutionary course of action for poor urban women: "The girls, realizing this inability on the part of their mothers, elated by that sense of independence which the first taste of self-support always brings, sheltered from observation during certain hours, are *almost as free from social control as is the traditional young man* who comes up from the country to take care of himself in a great city" (pp. 14–15, emphasis added).

The depiction of young women "almost as free" as young men would seem to embody the radical social change that Addams's economic analysis advocated—higher wages, better jobs, more leisure for athletics, and more discretion in choosing amusements. She gets all the way to this image of the unfettered, working-class female but then recoils.

Addams's speeches, essays, and books feature a community of voices, what her contemporary Mikhail Bakhtin called "dialogic writing," which gave her prose the sound of fiction. Her arguments about American culture come interlaced with stories from the common road, and she persuades readers to trust that she will faithfully relay her actual conversations with the working-class immigrants of Halsted Street. The problem for Jane Addams in writing on this topic is that she could not be convincing about her encounters with "fallen women." Allen Davis has observed that she did not actually talk with young women who had gone "wrong."[16] Without firsthand knowledge (and without secondhand knowledge across the sexual border of middle-class respectability) how could she tell the story with credibility? That limitation made her wary of writing this book in the first place.

As *Twenty Years at Hull-House* made its way into readers' hands, editors and publishers were eager to secure Jane Addams's next book, especially one that explored the most sensational, even lurid, topic in America before the outbreak of war in Europe. George P. Brett, her editor at Macmillan, wrote in October of 1910 that Edward Marsh "would probably be very glad to publish it [the book]."[17] Addams held him off for a year, fearing that he would announce a publication date that would require her to write more quickly than she thought possible or wise. "I am quite sure that I can do nothing in regard to the other book during the winter beyond collecting material," she insisted, cautioning "I am afraid we must regard its publication as problematical."[18] Marsh urged her to focus a new book "on the problem of the girls in large cities," flattering her by adding that she would give the topic "a serious and unsensational treatment."[19]

A month later, Brett nudged her again for "another book which I think is much needed, on the position of young girls and women when they first come to the city to take up work in the great manufacturing and mercantile establishments."[20] Addams, who was moving in his direction, replied, "[W]e are getting together a great deal of interesting material in connection with the Juvenile Protective Association" even as she warned him not to announce the book because there was "danger of over-statement" on the topic of girls alone in the city.[21]

Publishing in the United States mushroomed after 1891, when international copyrights were established, ending the cheap reprinting of books by European writers. The work of American authors became a good buy. According to John Tebbel, the gentlemanly editors of the late-nineteenth century—George Palmer Putnam, Charles Scribner, Henry Houghton, and James T. Fields—were followed by a new, more competitive group, men such as Frank Doubleday, Walter Hines Page (who encouraged Addams to write her autobiography), and George P. Brett.[22] Brett, who had sought out Addams and then struggled to retain her, offered her advances and patiently suggested new projects, explaining from the start of their relationship that she would do well by keeping their publishing marriage together.

Literary agents were popular after 1900, as best-selling writers commanded the attention of publishers. Unlike other successful authors, however, Jane Addams insisted on making deals for herself. She also marketed her writing in more than one place, which enhanced her readership and garnered income, and her letters are full of artful negotiations with Brett and the editors of popular magazines.

Addams planned an especially long summer away from Chicago in 1911, and by April George Brett had learned of her intentions. "Someone told us the other day that you were expecting to take a long summer holiday this year," he began his spring letter, pointing out again that the vacation would allow her "opportunity for the getting together of the material for the book."[23] She responded coolly, "I hope to do some work this summer upon the book concerning girls in the city, but as I wrote before I am quite unwilling to have it announced because I am not sure that the material which I have will be of any value."[24] The book would be her most controversial one. Addams could hardly take up the subject of female sexual vulnerability without raising eyebrows. Even as she dragged her heels with Brett, she was moving ahead with Samuel S. McClure and discussing magazine publication of material from the book.

An irony at the core of the book on women in the city is that Jane Addams left Chicago to write it. Throughout her life, she was a literary person, although she usually found the time and energy to write only as she retreated from Hull-House to the northern suburb of Waukegan, or to Mackinac Island, or still later to Bar Harbor and Hot Springs. Her letters of 1911 are her first to mention living at Hull's Cove. In an invitation to Lillian Wald, founder of the Henry Street Settlement in New York City, she urged, "see me in my house at Bar Harbor."[25]

It is clear from her correspondence that the natural beauty of the Maine coast eased her into writing, even as the cultural landscape of Chicago stimulated her literary imagination. "McClure is hurrying me for the first 'reading' of my stuff," she told a colleague, Grace Abbott. "I have quite enjoyed writing it altho the subject is grisly—I have tried to hide it, under the title 'A New Conscience and an Ancient Evil.'"[26]

Hide it indeed! Through the late summer of 1911 she continued to bargain with both McClure and Marsh to secure publication, first in the magazine and then in a book. There is every indication that she relished making literary deals. Her Macmillan royalty statement that year stood at $3,922.10, including the sale of 407 copies of *Democracy and Social Ethics* (1902), 409 copies of *Newer Ideals of Peace* (1907), a hefty 2,756 of *The Spirit of Youth and the City Streets* (1909), and a first-year sale of 16,877 of *Twenty Years at Hull-House* (1910). Little wonder that the publishers competed for her next effort. As she explained to Edward Marsh, the article on the social evil, promised to McClure, had grown into a book of seven chapters. "As I begun [*sic*] it with the magazine article in mind, I have tried to keep the phraseology and tone, so that it might be read by the general public without embarrassment."[27] She offered the chapters for his perusal, and George Brett responded that they would accept the book without having read the chapters, "sure of a wide reading" for anything she had written.[28] What she wanted to do was publish the book in March 1912 and the magazine articles by November 1911, allowing enough time between to avoid a problem with copyright law.

Brett and Marsh wrangled over the proper venue for a book that, whatever the tone she used in whatever veiled language, promised to be a surprisingly sexy project. Hoping to keep the material for himself, Brett cautioned Addams that the material was unsuitable for a magazine. At the same time, McClure urged her to publish in his magazine, where a readership of five hundred thousand families would surely boost book sales. McClure playfully wooed Addams even as he shrewdly made his case. "I am setting up nights for the manuscript," he joked.[29] When she finally sent the manuscript, he pounced: "I feel that it is just the sort of material that I want for my magazine."[30] Unlike Brett and Marsh, McClure read the manuscript and offered to use it all over five months, from December 1911 through April 1912, well past the March publication that Brett hoped to secure. McClure also offered Addams $1,000 for the series and praised the "singular nobility of tone" of her writing.

Two days later Marsh's next letter arrived, advising against serialization in the magazine. "I doubt whether they are the kind of readers you want," he warned, because the sensational subject could prove dangerous to her reputation as a writer. Realizing the implication of that, however, he pulled back: "Of course, your handling of the subject is at the farthest remove from the sensational."[31] Marsh worked to dissuade Addams from giving away the material before Macmillan could sell the book. Her goal, after all, was to garner as much money and as many readers as possible.

Addams chastised McClure for offering only $1,000, writing hastily in pencil that he should consider the effect on a writer who is "unduly compensated" for her work and suggesting that he return the manuscript. "*The American* paid me more for my articles than you offer and I shall have to say 1500.00 for the series of five," she insisted.[32] Of course, a deal was struck with both men, who were equally eager not to offend her. Addams arranged for the Macmillan book to be published in March and for *McClure's* articles in November and December. McClure even offered to extend her deadline to September 11 if she would tell him the number of words he should leave space for on the pages. "[P]lease do not fail me," he implored.[33] Brett, too, humored her by promising to use a union binding shop, something he had neglected to do for her last book.

During this prolonged negotiation, Addams seemed at home in Bar Harbor and relaxed as well in her writing. She invited Florence Kelley to have a look at the "little book." Alice Hamilton wrote that Addams's portraits of poor women were "awfully good and illuminating, especially Olga's."[34] Addams, who found comfort in friends, also wrote to Lillian Wald that she was "so anxious to have [her] see this beautiful island."[35] During a long separation from her partner Mary Rozet Smith, recuperating in Hot Springs from a variety of ailments, Addams gently reassured, "Dearest—I do wish you could really believe that I would rather be with you than anyone else."[36] She sent the magazine articles to McClure from Bar Harbor and later, during the winter months, revised the book's manuscript in Colorado. As she vacationed there with Mary Smith, Addams read Dreiser's *Jennie Gerhardt*.

In *A New Conscience and an Ancient Evil*, Addams, who often spoke through her characters to give validity to an argument, does not rhetorically become a fallen woman. What she promises readers instead is a single voice. "[The book] endeavors to present the contributory causes, as they have become registered in my consciousness through a long

residence in a crowded city quarter" (p. 6). The young women in a series of vignettes as much from fiction as fact are all angels of the slum
and akin to heroines of white slavery narratives: gullible, unskilled,
uneducated, confused, powerless, inarticulate, and very much in need
of a mother. The mature narrative voice, that of the professional settlement worker, constructs an argument from a series of "grisly" stories.

Often no more than children, "slum angels" enter Chicago as innocents and fall under the weight of forces they never understand.
Marie, "a French girl, the daughter of a Breton stone mason, so old and
poor that he was obliged to take her from her convent school at the age
of twelve years," is accosted on the way to buy milk by a procurer, who
plies her with sweets and pictures of showgirls (p. 9). Once she has been
thus lured to Chicago, she is pressed into prostitution, earning $250 a
week for a pimp and nothing for herself. Olga, whose mother returns
to Sweden, is left in Chicago to fend for herself, but "a friendless girl
of such striking beauty could not escape the machinations of those who
profit by the sale of girls" (p. 15). Driven mad by her pursuers, Olga is
arrested and at the point of being sent to prison when she is rescued
by the Juvenile Protective Association. Her story reinforces Addams's
belief that "no one can safely live without companionship and affection" (p. 16), without the support and direction, that is, of other women,
especially social workers. In yet other cases, a young factory girl from
a Bohemian family living in Milwaukee is tricked by a promise of marriage; a Polish woman, destitute after her mother dies, mimics the behavior of neighborhood prostitutes; and a fifteen-year-old American
comes to Chicago from a small town to work in a department store in
order to keep her elderly parents and sickly brother alive, only to be
forced to moonlight as a prostitute.

In every configuration, the girl appears in Addams's evolutionary
model as an urban primitive: "Because she is of the first generation of
girls which has stood alone in the midst of trade, she is clinging and
timid" (p. 31). A young woman may wish to assert independence: "We
all know that the American girl has grown up in the belief that the world
is hers from which to choose, that there is ordinarily no limit to her
ambition or to her definition of success" (p. 31). Such exaggerated self-
confidence, however, is dangerous, as Addams warns in example after
example. The sexual "pander" or "cadet" is always around, hovering

everywhere. Society, Addams concludes, must keep girls in school for an additional six and a half years—not a bad idea if education were the goal, but it was not.

Addams assumes—and here the eroticized transgressor loses her power as a symbol of social change—that poor women eventually want to become wives and mothers: "the great business of youth is securing a mate, as the young instinctively understand" (p. 76). Nowhere does Addams argue for the movement of working-class women into professional life to become nurses or settlement-house workers or eugenics engineers. They are to be protected by the strong moral arms of the new professional class of women who come from colleges and universities, the types of professionals whom Addams gathered at Hull-House. Her answer to patriarchal sexual exploitation, as it turns out, is matriarchal protection arising from the "primitive maternal instinct" to nurture and defend (p. 87). As she delineated the difference, "The chastity of the modern woman of self-directed activity and of a varied circle of interests, which gives her an acquaintance with many men as well as women, has therefore a new value and importance in the establishment of social standards" (p. 96).

The modern urban woman—and Addams considered herself one—was to arrive in a city as an observer, a useful builder of social order, and especially a writer. Christopher Lasch, who admires Addams's prose, notes that her stories of city life "describe how it felt to stumble upon a whole realm of social existence that the conventions of middle-class culture and education had completely concealed."[37]

Addams was able to write about her experiences in the city because she could distance herself from the social work she and others designed. Jean Bethke Elshtain labels her a "public intellectual" and sees Hull-House as a cultural and intellectual center that attracted academics, especially those at the University of Chicago, who were defining sociology.[38] Louis Menand focuses on male intellectuals (Oliver Wendell Holmes, William James, Charles Sanders Peirce, and John Dewey) yet connects Jane Addams to other pragmatists. He also makes a neat point about her as a social and professional observer: "The moment Addams had this insight into the nature of her own work was the moment she ceased being a do-gooder, or even a reformer, and became a social scientist. She became the sociologist of her own profession: she was the first sociologist of social work."[39]

As a sociologist, Addams perceived the distance between the economic vulnerability of working-class women and the economic independence of the female social worker. Margit Stange has it right when she describes the new professional woman: "Remaining erect at her public post, she must endure public exposure without falling into commodification, repeatedly fulfilling her civic obligations while still guarding her chastity."[40] Addams and Florence Dedrick made the same point: "As woman, however, fulfills her civic obligations while still guarding her chastity, she will be in position as never before to uphold the 'single standard,' demanding that men shall add the personal virtues to their performance of public duties" (p. 96). A city woman must avoid even a hint of sexuality and thus serve as a model, even to urban males.

Walter Lippmann puzzled over the tone of *A New Conscience and an Ancient Evil,* calling it "an hysterical book, just because the real philosophical basis of Miss Addams' thinking was not deliberate enough to withstand the shock of a poignant horror."[41] Allen Davis also pronounced it "an hysterical book, also sentimental and naive."[42] He complained that Addams took up the issue of sexual slavery because it was a popular topic that would heighten her public image as "Saint Jane." Davis also charged that she bullied *McClure's* and Macmillan into paying her twice for the same material.

If we were to strip the book of its "poignant horror" (by which term Lippmann meant the stories of sexual slavery) and follow the logic of Addams's argument about poor women and work, we would find an economic analysis closely paralleling Charlotte Perkins Gilman's in *Women and Economics* (1899). The two women met in California in 1894 at an annual meeting of the Federation of Woman's Clubs, Gilman claiming Addams as a friend and advocate. Addams found the meetings themselves uninspiring, and yet she stayed in contact with her new friend, inviting her to stay at Hull-House as Gilman was gracelessly evicted from California for "debt and failure." Gilman traveled from California to Chicago in 1896 and spent three months at Hull-House with Addams. Their discussions that summer resulted in a curious cross-pollination, as each woman borrowed ideas from the other.

Gilman, although gratified by the intellectual audience at Hull-House, found visceral contact with the poor repulsive. Well before the obligatory six-month residency was over, Addams arranged for Gilman to run a settlement house on the North Side of Chicago in a neighborhood known as "Little Hell." Gilman considered the grim prospect in her autobiography: "The loathly river flowed sluggishly near by, thick and ill-smelling; Goose Island lay black in the slow stream." The social ideal of living among the poor placed her in a toxic environment: "Everywhere a heavy dinginess, low, dark brick factories and gloomy wooden dwellings often below the level of the street; foul plank sidewalks, rotten and full of holes; black mud underfoot, damp soot drifting steadily down over everything." Gilman turned the work of running the settlement over to Helen Campbell—"my interest was in all humanity, not merely the under side of it, in sociology, not social pathology"—and spent the next years traveling and lecturing.[43] Because she wrote about sociology, Gilman could address the economic and social problems women faced in the city without having to dirty her hands.

Gilman was thinking about her sociological treatise *Women and Economics* and pleased to have Addams's approval of the project: "She is really impressed with the big new idea. To have her see it is a great help," she noted in her diary.[44] The study compares prostitution to marriage because both provide payment for the comfort of sex. "Because of the economic dependence of the human female on her mate," Gilman theorized, "she is modified to sex to an excessive degree."[45] A woman supposedly transmits the "morbid tendency to excess" to her children, causing devolution of the species. In stories about white slavery that appear in her later fiction, Gilman focused on the relationship of mother to son. The heroine of "His Mother," for example, launches an assault on the sex trade: "She visited the night courts and learned how young girls are treated there; she read the reports of the Vice Commissions, of various reformatory institutions, of the national and international societies how engaged in rescue or preventive work."[46] In her research, she discovers that her own son has become a "pander," forcing his brutish attentions on a young shop girl. "He locked the door as he brought her in; he laid the helpless form down on his bed, standing a moment with a sneering smile," as Gilman imagines the scene of debauchery. To his consternation, the eyes he encounters are the gray eyes of his mother, who is acting as a spy and willing to turn him over to the police, "present to take him away."[47] Gilman is fascinated with sex as a social and biological force that attracts and repels. Ironically, however, the heavy hand of the sociologist flattens the power of her fiction.

Addams's study of the sexual behavior of poor and working-class women owes much to Gilman's analysis. Sex becomes a commodity in the public square as surely as it does in the private sphere, yet for Addams a vulnerable young woman must seek the moral sanctity of marriage. An educated, upper-middle-class woman, however, might avoid marriage altogether by finding a professional equivalent or substitute that provides a comfortable living, but beyond that putatively asexual existence she dares not venture.

One of Addams's stories, an example from the Juvenile Protective Association, reads much like the other fiction of her day. "A surprising number of country girls have been either brought to Chicago under false pretences," she begins in lines that sound like no writer more than Theodore Dreiser, "or have been decoyed into an evil life very soon after their arrival in the city" (p. 66). Clifford Roe, she adds, believed that more than half of the recruited girls in the city were from farms or small towns, just the sort of places that Dreiser chronicles. In Addams's story, a pretty girl defends her fall into prostitution with a tale of seduction and betrayal. "This girl had been a hotel chambermaid in an Iowa town where many of the traveling patrons of the hotel had made love to her, one of them occasionally offering her protection if she would leave with him" (p. 66). After repeated entreaties, she travels with him to Seattle and then to Chicago, where she believes the pleasure is over. Fearful of returning to her small town in disgrace and charmed by the idleness of the city, she becomes a prostitute and is rescued by a policeman who takes her to the association. The man in question, "distractedly searching for her" (p. 67), arrives, marries her, and relieves Addams of further responsibility. What makes the country girl an easy mark, Addams argues, is the loss of the village gossip, who provided a reliable eye on community life and sexual activity. Once she is in the city, who will look out for an inexperienced girl and tell her story?

Theodore Dreiser had written to Addams as he reworked *Jennie Gerhardt,* urgently requesting that she write an article for *The Delineator* on the topic of the widow and her children, the issue that perplexed him. He was seeking a way to bring closure to his story and bring his fallen heroine back into the community. In the end, he placed her in "Sandwood," a suburb of lakeshore cottages north of Chicago. Her erotic energy is exhausted, and her lover has died as well as their daughter. As a widow of sorts, she adopts two children and embodies the sanitized safety of the suburbs, where second-generation Americans were being absorbed into bland patterns of economic and political conformity. As Elizabeth Ewen explains, "Successful adoption of the suburban consumer ideal meant hiding all traces of one's roots. All telltale signs of the old way were smothered."[48] Smothering immigrant culture may have soothed Dreiser as he made his way into American literary society. While Jane Addams revised her manuscript of *A New Conscience and an Ancient Evil* in the winter of 1912, however, she read his second novel and remarked to friends that she did not find his "bed of roses" ending credible.[49]

Addams was herself looking for a suburban retreat to share with other social workers and their working-class urban neighbors. With money from the estate of Joseph Tilton Bowen, Louise de Koven Bowen's husband, and a $50,000 gift from Julius Rosenwald, the Chicago settlement bought a version of Sandwood in Waukegan, Illinois. There they established the Joseph T. Bowen Country Club in June 1912, a natural landscape that seemed untouched by human design. The motto of the club was "secure from the slow stain of the world's contagion."

The sexual energy of the city left Addams in as much doubt as it did Dreiser about the effects of the world's "slow stain." She didn't buy the roses of Sandwood at the end of Dreiser's story, perhaps because she found Jennie's ease in joining middle-class society unconvincing. Too, the woman working her own way through the white slavery narrative had yet to find a better way to end the tale. A slum angel could not escape into an independent life; she could only find shelter at the hands of the nurturing professional women of the settlement house. They would initiate her into manners, mores, and values acceptable to the American middle class. Dreiser's novel and Addams's narrative may well have calmed readers eager to deny the social change that poor, rural, and immigrant women brought with them to Chicago.

Macmillan advertised *A New Conscience and an Ancient Evil* in language that fell just short of the rhetoric of lurid exposés. "A work to be seriously pondered by every serious man and woman," the copy read. "Actual experiences of those who have investigated the 'white-slave' traffic, and often the stories of girls who have been drawn into the net—are the things of which Miss Addams' book is made." Moreover, it was "absolutely frank in its treatment of the social evil, startling in its revelations, judicious in its suggestions and sympathetic in its viewpoint." The advertisement of April 17, 1912, teetered between sensational and judicious rhetoric. The audience for the book differed, as Brett predicted, from that of the series in *McClure's* magazine, but both publishing venues attracted the curious, many of whom wrote to Addams.

Young female readers felt camaraderie with her, and many were prompted to write intimately. Charlotte Howett Lansey, for example, wrote a mash note of sorts. "It is impossible for one woman to make a declaration of adoration for another," she declared, "and yet this is exactly what I am doing."[50] Phoebe Willets saw the sensationalism of the white slavery narrative as literary sightseeing. "Your book is another example of this method of money getting; is it not?" she queried. Willets placed Addams's own sexual experience under scrutiny and noted that she had never "been married to a good man and attained a normal view of certain relations."[51] Another letter from Willets arrived the next week, this one even more admonitory: "'Miss Addams is beginning to see the *world* through Hull-House *windows*' and I feel you should be asked to consider if this is be not *true?*" As Addams gained celebrity, Willets charged, she lost the ability to judge her own writing. "You are *too certain* of general acclamation," Willets continued, adding, "You do not see your limitations, perhaps because of flattery."[52] Willets showed her hand at the end of letter when she condemned Addams's efforts in the suffrage movement as evil and hysterical.

A typical complaint among magazine readers concerned Addams's use of "cadet" as a term for a young man in the sex trade. She received a flood of protests from military men, who thought of themselves as cadets. Charles N. Sawyer, for example, noted, "It is with a sense of pain that I have of late seen it used in anything but a manly sense."[53] The letter signals how quickly Addams would fall from grace when she opposed World War I. "And with more pain," Sawyer warned, "have I found it in the articles of a noble woman whose life has been devoted to the service of others." As many readers perceived her to be openly political, they became critical of her as a writer.

Editors, however, noting the strong sale of her books, pursued Addams with more energy. Elizabeth G. Jorgan of *Harper's* (the publisher that had bowdlerized Dreiser's fiction) offered Addams $200 for 2,500 words for a special Christmas issue featuring women authors. The suggested topic was "What Can the Average Woman Do for the Community?"[54] Ralph Fletcher Seymour wanted to publish her next book, one on suffrage, perhaps, or on anything at all that she chose, and followed up with a letter suggesting a brief book of five thousand words, to be sold for fifty cents a copy. *Women's Wear* invited Addams to write a column that would take up the issue of women's clothing in the work place. George Matthew Adams proposed a syndicated column or "brief talk" of four to six hundred words daily except Sunday. Macmillan sent her yearly account of $1,728.29 on sales for all her books, including 4,095 copies of *A New Conscience and an Ancient Evil*. Ever mindful of her summer writing habit, George Brett began the ritual in June 1912 by acknowledging that the book on white slavery had evoked "wide comment almost entirely favourable."[55]

A New Conscience and an Ancient Evil hit a nerve with readers willing to ponder Addams's suggestion that young women in modern cities might find themselves "almost as free from social control as is the traditional young man" (p. 14). H. H. Herbst from the Huron Valley Building and Savings Association read the magazine version and took Addams to task on the issue of frankness. "So far as I can learn, there is but slight difference in the sexual passions of boys and girls from sixteen years up," he observed, adding that it would "appall the ordinary reader" to learn how many boys and girls between the ages of fifteen and twenty-two, "school mates, companions and ordinary acquaintances," indulge in unlawful sexual intercourse. In Herbst's experience, males were no more likely than female to be sexual aggressors: "They enter into such relations thoughtlessly, spurred on by passion, at times favorable to the act."[56] The sexually inquisitive and aggressive Dreiser sisters, languishing in Terre Haute and yearning to try their luck in Chicago, may have been more typical than anyone wanted to say.

What agitated B. A. Behrend of the Institute of Electrical Engineers was the idea that illicit sex might leave a woman relatively unscarred.[57] He wanted Addams to know about a twenty-seven-year-old woman who was president of her church society, vice president of her college fraternity, a teacher at a women's college, and a seemingly respectable member of the community. Behrend knew, however, that for five years she had an affair with a young, Harvard-trained lawyer, and during that time they had engaged in acts "which included every indecent practice known to degenerates like those practiced by Stanford White." More astonishing to Behrend was a medical report: "A physical examination showed that owing to the unnatural nature of the practices, no physical injury had been done to her." Moreover, the young woman, seven years later, appeared mentally and intellectually normal—and not to say professionally successful. Behrend confided to Addams that he had read letters written during the affair, although "the offending man had used such gross immoral expressions and such utterly vile degenerate language that even the hardened detectives blushed with shame and declined to act, stating that no woman could be so innocent and ignorant as not to know the moral wrong of such matters." The "fallen" woman, Behrends concluded, had a Jekyll and Hyde personality, and he admitted that he continued to introduce her into polite society. Perhaps hoping for expiation, he sent Jane Addams a check for $50: "Please accept it as a sacrifice on the altar of human suffering."

Behrend's letter suggests the strong desire for sexual knowledge that readers of white slavery narratives must have felt, a fact coupled with perplexity about what to do with such knowledge. The women were indeed in the city, and few were angels.

NOTES

1. Florence Mabel Dedrick, "Our Sister of the Street," *Fighting the Traffic in Young Girls; or, The War on the White Slave Trade* (Chicago: G. S. Ball, 1910), 107.

2. Jane Addams, *The Spirit of Youth and the City Streets* (New York: Macmillan, 1909), 8.

3. Princess Alice, consort of Alexander, Prince of Teck, to Jane Addams, July 10,

1910, in *The Jane Addams Papers, 1860–1960*, ed. Mary Lynn McCree Bryan (Ann Arbor: University Microfilms International, 1984), 5–1220. All letters and manuscripts used in this introduction can be found in the Jane Addams Papers Project (JAPP), eighty-two reels of microfilm that comprise her papers, both personal and professional, and papers associated with Hull-House.

4. Dedrick, "Our Sister of the Street," 107.

5. Kathy Peiss, *Cheap Amusements: Working Women and Leisure in Turn-of-the-Century New York* (Philadelphia: Temple University Press, 1986). See Peiss, "'Charity Girls,' and City Pleasures: Historical Notes on Working-Class Sexuality, 1880–1920," in *Passion and Power: Sexuality in History,* ed. Kathy Peiss and Christina Simmons (Philadelphia: Temple University Press, 1989), 57–69; and George Kneeland, *Commercialized Prostitution in New York City* (New York: Century, 1913).

6. Judith Walkowitz, *City of Dreadful Delight: Narratives of Sexual Danger in Late-Victorian London* (Chicago: University of Chicago Press, 1992), 21; see also Kathleen Barry, *The Prostitution of Sexuality* (New York: New York University Press, 1995), 91–113. Barry agrees with Judith R. Walkowitz, author of "Male Vice and Female Virtue: Feminism and the Politics of Prostitution in Nineteenth-Century Britain," in *Powers of Desire: The Politics of Sexuality,* ed. Ann Snitow, Christine Stansell, and Sharon Thompson (New York: Monthly Review Press, 1983), 420–33. For a contemporary account, see Josephine Butler, *Personal Reminiscences of a Great Crusader* (1911, repr. Westport: Hyperion, 1976), 221.

7. Katherine Joslin, "Slum Angels: The White-Slave Narrative in Theodore Dreiser's *Sister Carrie*," in *Women, America, and Movement: Narratives of Relocation,* ed. Susan L. Roberson (Columbia: University of Missouri Press, 1998), 106–20.

8. Teresa Billington-Greig quoted in Barry, *Prostitution of Sexuality,* 117. See Ruth Rosen, *The Lost Sisterhood: Prostitution in America, 1900–1918* (Baltimore: Johns Hopkins University Press, 1982); and Barbara Meil Hobson, *Uneasy Virtue: The Politics of Prostitution and the American Reform Tradition* (New York: Basic Books, 1987).

9. Emma Goldman, "The Traffic in Women," in *Red Emma Speaks: Selected Writings and Speeches by Emma Goldman,* ed. Alix Kates Shulman (New York: Random House, 1972), 145.

10. Rosen, *The Lost Sisterhood,* xvi.

11. The Vice Commission of Chicago, *The Social Evil in Chicago* (Chicago: Gunthorp-Warren Printing, 1911).

12. Carol Green Wilson, *Chinatown Quest* (San Francisco: California Historical Society, 1974). See also Kathleen Barry, *The Prostitution of Sexuality* (New York: New York University Press, 1995), 118.

13. Jeffrey Weeks, *Sex, Politics, and Society: The Regulation of Sexuality since 1800* (London: Longman, 1981).

14. Peter Stallybrass and Allon White, *The Politics and Poetics of Transgression* (Ithaca: Cornell University Press, 1986), 5.

15. Mark Connelly, *The Response to Prostitution in the Progressive Era* (Chapel

Hill: University of North Carolina Press, 1980), 22. Connelly reads the white-slave narrative as a jeremiad, a lament over the loss of agrarian values and an admission of guilt, a stage necessary for the acceptance of the social changes already evident in the twentieth-century city.

16. Allen F. Davis, *American Heroine: The Life and Legend of Jane Addams* (New York: Oxford University Press, 1973), 182.

17. George Brett to Jane Addams, Oct. 7, 1910, JAPP 5–1298.

18. Jane Addams to George Brett, Nov. 2, 1910, JAPP 5–1308.

19. Edward Marsh to Jane Addams, Nov. 30, 1910, JAPP 5–1357.

20. George Brett to Jane Addams, Jan., 1911, JAPP 6–0027.

21. Jane Addams to George Brett, Jan. 13, 1911, JAPP 6–0047.

22. John Tebbel, *A History of Book Publishing in the United States*, 4 vols. (New York: R. R. Bowker, 1972–81), 3:307.

23. George Brett to Jane Addams, April 13, 1911, JAPP 6–0224.

24. Jane Addams to George Brett, April 17, 1911, JAPP 6–0233.

25. Jane Addams to Lillian Wald, May 3, 1911, JAPP 6–0284.

26. Jane Addams to Grace Abbott, July 28, 1911, JAPP 6–0380.

27. Jane Addams to Edward Marsh, July 31, 1911, JAPP 6–0386.

28. George Brett to Jane Addams, Aug. 2, 1911, JAPP 6–0391.

29. Samuel S. McClure to Jane Addams, Aug. 8, 1911, JAPP 6–0401.

30. Samuel S. McClure to Jane Addams, Aug. 15, 1911, JAPP 6–0418.

31. Edward Marsh to Jane Addams, Aug. 17, 1911, JAPP 6–0423.

32. Jane Addams to Samuel S. McClure, Aug. 21, 1911, JAPP 6–0426.

33. Samuel S. McClure to Jane Addams, Sept. 1, 1911, JAPP 6–0439.

34. Alice Hamilton to Jane Addams, Aug. 14, 1911, JAPP 6–0408.

35. Jane Addams to Lillian Wald, Aug. 11, 1911, JAPP 6–0403.

36. Jane Addams to Mary Rozet Smith, Aug. 24, 1911, JAPP 6–0430.

37. Christopher Lasch, *The Social Thought of Jane Addams*, American Heritage Series, Leonard W. Levy and Alfred Young, general editors (Indianapolis: Bobbs-Merrill, 1965), xxvi.

38. Jean Bethke Elshtain, *Jane Addams and the Dream of American Democracy: A Life* (New York: Basic Books, 2001).

39. Louis Menand, *The Metaphysical Club: A Story of Ideas in America* (New York: Farrar Straus and Giroux, 2001), 312.

40. Margit Stange, *Personal Property: Wives, White Slaves, and the Market in Women* (Baltimore: Johns Hopkins University Press, 1998), 137.

41. Walter Lippmann, *A Preface to Politics*, quoted in Davis, *American Heroine*, 78.

42. Davis, *American Heroine*, 183.

43. Charlotte Perkins Gilman, *The Living of Charlotte Perkins Gilman: An Autobiography*, with an introduction by Zona Gale (1935, repr. New York: Harper and Row, 1975), 184–85. For a longer discussion of the literary relationship between Addams and Gilman, see Janet Beer and Katherine Joslin, "Diseases of the Body Politic: White Slavery in Jane Addams' *A New Conscience and an Ancient Evil* and

Selected Short Stories by Charlotte Perkins Gilman," *Journal of American Studies* 33 (April 1999): 1–18.

44. Gilman, *The Living of Charlotte Perkins Gilman,* 229.

45. Charlotte Perkins Gilman, *Women and Economics* (1898, repr. New York: Harpers, 1966), 95.

46. Ann Lane, ed., *The Charlotte Perkins Gilman Reader* (London: Women's Press, 1981), 122.

47. Lane, ed., *The Charlotte Perkins Gilman Reader,* 122.

48. Elizabeth Ewen, *Immigrant Women in the Land of Dollars: Life and Culture on the Lower East Side, 1890–1925* (New York: Monthly Review Press, 1985), 268.

49. Jane Addams to Mary Rozet Smith, Feb. 21, 1912, JAPP 6–831.

50. Charlotte Howett Lansey to Jane Addams, Jan. 27, 1912, JAPP 6–798.

51. Phoebe Willets to Jane Addams, July 11, 1912, JAPP 6–1114.

52. Phoebe Willets to Jane Addams, July 17, 1912, JAPP 6–1128.

53. Charles N. Sawyer to Jane Addams, March 19, 1912, JAPP 6–879.

54. Elizabeth G. Jorgan to Jane Addams, April 30, 1912, JAPP 6–961.

55. George Brett to Jane Addams, June 15, 1912, JAPP 6–1062.

56. H. H. Herbst to Jane Addams, Jan. 20, 1912, JAPP 6–0779.

57. B. A. Behrend to Jane Addams, May 22, 1912, JAPP 6–1006.

A New Conscience
and an Ancient Evil

Preface

✍ The following material, much of which has been published in *McClure's Magazine,* was written, not from the point of view of the expert, but because of my own need for a counter-knowledge to a bewildering mass of information which came to me through the Juvenile Protective Association of Chicago. The reports which its twenty field officers daily brought to its main office adjoining Hull-House became to me a revelation of the dangers implicit in city conditions and of the allurements which are designedly placed around many young girls in order to draw them into an evil life.

As head of the Publication Committee, I read the original documents in a series of special investigations made by the Association on dance halls, theatres, amusement parks, lake excursion boats, petty gambling, the home surroundings of one hundred Juvenile Court children and the records of four thousand parents who clearly contributed to the delinquency of their own families. The Association also collected the personal histories of two hundred department-store girls, of two hundred factory girls, of two hundred immigrant girls, of two hundred office girls, and of girls employed in one hundred hotels and restaurants.

While this experience was most distressing, I was, on the other hand, much impressed and at times fairly startled by the large and diversified number of people to whom the very existence of the white slave traffic had become unendurable and who promptly responded to any appeal made on behalf of its victims. City officials, policemen, judges, attorneys, employers, trades unionists, physicians, teachers, newly arrived immigrants, clergymen, railway officials, and newspaper men, as under a profound sense of compunction, were unsparing of time and effort when given an opportunity to assist an individual girl, to promote legislation designed for her protection, or to establish institutions for her rescue.

I therefore venture to hope that in serving my own need I may also serve the need of a rapidly growing public when I set down for rational consideration the temptations surrounding multitudes of young people and when I assemble, as best I may, the many indications of a new conscience, which in various directions is slowly gathering strength and which we may soberly hope will at last successfully array itself against this incredible social wrong, ancient though it may be.

Jane Addams
Hull-House, Chicago

1

An Analogy

☙ In every large city throughout the world thousands of women are so set aside as outcasts from decent society that it is considered an impropriety to speak the very word which designates them. Lecky calls this type of woman "the most mournful and the most awful figure in history": he says that "she remains, while creeds and civilizations rise and fall, the eternal sacrifice of humanity, blasted for the sins of the people." But evils so old that they are imbedded in man's earliest history have been known to sway before an enlightened public opinion and in the end to give way to a growing conscience, which regards them first as a moral affront and at length as an utter impossibility. Thus the generation just before us, our own fathers, uprooted the enormous upas of slavery, "the tree that was literally as old as the race of man," although slavery doubtless had its beginnings in the captives of man's earliest warfare, even as this existing evil thus originated.

Those of us who think we discern the beginnings of a new conscience in regard to this twin of slavery, as old and outrageous as slavery itself and even more persistent, find a possible analogy between certain civic, philanthropic and educational efforts directed against the very existence of this social evil and similar organized efforts which preceded the overthrow of slavery in America. Thus, long before slavery was finally declared illegal, there were international regulations of its traffic, state and federal legislation concerning its extension, and many extra legal attempts to control its abuses; quite as we have the international regulations concerning the white slave traffic, the state and interstate legislation for its repression, and an extra legal power in connection with it so universally given to the municipal police that the possession of this power has become one of the great sources of corruption in every American city.

Before society was ready to proceed against the institution of slavery as such, groups of men and women by means of the underground railroad cherished and educated individual slaves; it is scarcely necessary to point out the similarity to the rescue homes and preventive associations which every great city contains.

It is always easy to overwork an analogy, and yet the economist who for years insisted that slave labor continually and arbitrarily limited the wages of free labor and was therefore a detriment to national wealth was a forerunner of the economist of to-day who points out the economic basis of the social evil, the connection between low wages and despair, between over-fatigue and the demand for reckless pleasure.

Before the American nation agreed to regard slavery as unjustifiable from the standpoint of public morality, an army of reformers, lecturers, and writers set forth its enormity in a never-ceasing flow of invective, of appeal, and of portrayal concerning the human cruelty to which the system lent itself. We can discern the scouts and outposts of a similar army advancing against this existing evil: the physicians and sanitarians who are committed to the task of ridding the race from contagious diseases, the teachers and lecturers who are appealing to the higher morality of thousands of young people; the growing literature, not only biological and didactic, but of a popular type more closely approaching "Uncle Tom's Cabin."

Throughout the agitation for the abolition of slavery in America, there were statesmen who gradually became convinced of the political and moral necessity of giving to the freedman the protection of the ballot. In this current agitation there are at least a few men and women who would extend a greater social and political freedom to all women if only because domestic control has proved so ineffectual.

We may certainly take courage from the fact that our contemporaries are fired by social compassions and enthusiasms, to which even our immediate predecessors were indifferent. Such compunctions have ever manifested themselves in varying degrees of ardor through different groups in the same community. Thus among those who are newly aroused to action in regard to the social evil are many who would endeavor to regulate it and believe they can minimize its dangers, still larger numbers who would eliminate all trafficking of unwilling victims in connection with it, and yet others who believe that as a quasi-legal institution it may be absolutely abolished. Perhaps the analogy to the abolition of slavery is most striking in that these groups, in their varying points of view, are like those earlier associations which differed widely in regard to chattel slavery. Only the so-called extremists, in the first instance, stood for abolition and they were continually told that what they proposed was clearly impossible. The legal and commercial obstacles, bulked large, were placed before them and it was confidently asserted that the blame for the historic existence of slavery lay deep within human nature itself. Yet gradually all of these associations reached the point of view of the abolitionist and before the war was over even the most lukewarm unionist saw no other solution of the nation's difficulty. Some such gradual conversion to the point of view of abolition is the experience of every society or group of people who seriously face the difficulties and complications of the social evil. Certainly all the national organizations—the National Vigilance Committee, the American Purity Federation, the Alliance for the Suppression and Prevention of the White Slave Traffic and many others— stand for the final abolition of commercialized vice. Local vice commissions, such as the able one recently appointed in Chicago, although composed of members of varying beliefs in regard to the possibility of control and regulation, united in the end in recommending a law enforcement looking towards final abolition. Even the most sceptical of Chicago citizens, after reading the fearless document, shared the hope of the commission that "the city, when aroused to the truth, would instantly rebel against the social evil in all its phases." A similar recommendation of ultimate abolition was recently made unanimous by the Minneapolis vice commission after the conversion of many of its members. Doubtless all of the national societies have before them a task only less gigantic than that faced by those earlier associations in America for the suppression of slavery, although it may be legitimate to remind them that the best-known anti-slavery society in America was organized by the New England abolitionists in 1836, and only thirty-six years later, in 1872, was formally disbanded because its object had been accomplished. The long struggle ahead of these newer associations will doubtless claim its martyrs and its heroes, has indeed already claimed them during the last thirty years. Few righteous causes have escaped baptism with blood; nevertheless, to paraphrase Lincoln's speech, if blood were exacted drop by drop in measure to the tears of anguished mothers and enslaved girls, the nation would still be obliged to go into the struggle.

Throughout this volume the phrase "social evil" is used to designate the sexual commerce permitted to exist in every large city, usually in a segregated district, wherein the chastity of women is bought and sold. Modifications of legal codes regarding marriage and divorce, moral judgments concerning the entire group of questions centering about illicit affection between men and women, are quite other questions which are not considered here. Such problems must always remain distinct from those of commercialized vice, as must the treatment of an irreducible minimum of prostitution, which will doubtless long exist, quite as society still retains an irreducible minimum of murders. This volume does not deal with the probable future of prostitution, and gives only such historical background as is necessary to understand the present situation. It endeavors to present the contributory causes, as they have become registered in my consciousness through a long residence in a crowded city quarter, and to state the indications, as I have seen them, of a new conscience with its many and varied manifestations.

Nothing is gained by making the situation better or worse than it is, nor in anywise different from what it is. This ancient evil is indeed social in the sense of community responsibility and can only be understood and at length remedied when we face the fact and measure the resources which may at length be massed against it. Perhaps the most striking indication that our generation has become the bearer of a new moral consciousness in regard to the existence of commercialized vice is the fact that the mere contemplation of it throws the more sensitive men and women among our contemporaries into a state of indignant revolt. It is doubtless an instinctive shrinking from this emotion and an unconscious dread that this modern sensitiveness will be outraged, which justifies to themselves so many moral men and women in their persistent ignorance of the subject. Yet one of the most obvious resources at our command, which might well be utilized at once, if it is to be utilized at all, is the overwhelming pity and sense of protection which the recent revelations in the white slave traffic have aroused for the thousands of young girls, many of them still children, who are yearly sacrificed to the "sins of the people." All of this emotion ought to be made of value, for quite as a state of emotion is invariably the organic preparation for action, so it is certainly true that no profound spiritual transformation can take place without it.

After all, human progress is deeply indebted to a study of imperfections, and the counsels of despair, if not full of seasoned wisdom, are at least fertile in suggestion and a desperate spur to action. Sympathetic knowledge is the only way of approach to any human problem, and the line of least resistance into the jungle of human wretchedness must always be through that region which is most thoroughly explored, not only by the information of the statistician, but by sympathetic understanding. We are daily attaining the latter through such authors as Sudermann and Elsa Gerusalem, who have enabled their readers to comprehend the so-called "fallen" woman through a skilful portrayal of the reaction of experience upon personality. Their realism has rescued her from the sentimentality surrounding an impossible Camille quite as their fellow-craftsmen in realism have replaced the weeping Amelias of the Victorian period by reasonable women transcribed from actual life.

The treatment of this subject in American literature is at present in the pamphleteering stage, although an ever-increasing number of short stories and novels deal with it. On the other hand, the plays through which Bernard Shaw constantly places the truth before the public in England as Brieux is doing for the public in France, produce in the spectators a disquieting sense that society is involved in commercialized vice and must speedily find a way out. Such writing is like the roll of the drum which announces the approach of the troops ready for action.

Some of the writers who are performing this valiant service are related to those great artists who in every age enter into a long struggle with existing social conditions, until after many years they change the outlook upon life for at least a handful of their contemporaries. Their readers find themselves no longer mere bewildered spectators of a given social wrong, but have become conscious of their own hypocrisy in regard to it, and they realize that a veritable horror, simply because it was hidden, had come to seem to them inevitable and almost normal.

Many traces of this first uneasy consciousness regarding the social evil are found in contemporary literature, for while the business of literature is revelation and not reformation, it may yet perform for the men and women now living that purification of the imagination and intellect which the Greeks believed to come through pity and terror.

Secure in the knowledge of evolutionary processes, we have learned to talk glibly of the obligations of race progress and of the possibility of racial degeneration. In this respect certainly we have a wider outlook than that possessed by our fathers, who so valiantly grappled with chattel slavery and secured its overthrow. May the new conscience gather force until men and women, acting under its sway, shall be constrained to eradicate this ancient evil!

2

Recent Legal Enactments

🕭 At the present moment even the least conscientious citizens agree that, first and foremost, the organized traffic in what has come to be called white slaves must be suppressed and that those traffickers who procure their victims for purely commercial purposes must be arrested and prosecuted. As it is impossible to rescue girls fraudulently and illegally detained, save through governmental agencies, it is naturally through the line of legal action that the most striking revelations of the white slave traffic have come. For the sake of convenience, we may divide this legal action into those cases dealing with the international trade, those with the state and interstate traffic, and the regulations with which the municipality alone is concerned.

First in value to the white slave commerce is the girl imported from abroad who from the nature of the case is most completely in the power of the trader. She is literally friendless and unable to speak the language and at last discouraged she makes no effort to escape. Many cases of the international traffic were recently tried in Chicago and the offenders convicted by the federal authorities. One of these cases, which attracted much attention throughout the country, was of Marie, a French girl, the daughter of a Breton stone mason, so old and poor that he was obliged to take her from her convent school at the age of twelve years. He sent her to Paris, where she became a little household drudge and nurse-maid, working from six in the morning until eight at night, and for three years sending her wages, which were about a franc a day, directly to her parents in the Breton village. One afternoon, as she was buying a bottle of milk at a tiny shop, she was engaged in conversation by a young man who invited her into a little *patisserie* where, after giving her some sweets, he introduced her to his friend, Monsieur Paret, who was gathering together a theatrical troupe to go to America. Paret showed her pictures of several young girls gorgeously arrayed and announcements of their coming tour, and Marie felt much flattered when it was intimated that she might join this brilliant company. After several clandestine meetings to perfect the plan, she left the city with Paret and a pretty French girl to sail for America with the rest of the so-called actors. Paret escaped detection by the immigration authorities in New York, through his ruse of the "Kinsella troupe," and took the girls directly to Chicago. Here they were placed in a disreputable house belonging to a man named Lair, who had advanced the money for their importation. The two French girls remained in this house for several months until it was raided by the police, when they were sent to separate houses. The records which were later brought into court show that at this time Marie was earning two hundred and fifty dollars a week, all of which she gave to her employers. In spite of this large monetary return she was often cruelly beaten, was made to do the household scrubbing, and was, of course, never allowed to leave the house. Furthermore, as one of the methods of retaining a reluctant girl is to put her hopelessly in debt and always to charge against her the expenses incurred in securing her, Marie as an imported girl had begun at once with the huge debt of the ocean journey for Paret and herself. In addition to this large sum she was charged, according to universal custom, with exorbitant prices for all the clothing she received and with any money which Paret chose to draw against her account. Later, when Marie contracted typhoid fever, she was sent for treatment to a public hospital and it was during her illness there, when a general investigation was made of the white slave traffic, that a federal officer visited her. Marie, who thought she was going to die, freely gave her testimony, which proved to be most valuable.

The federal authorities following up her statements at last located Paret in the city prison at Atlanta, Georgia, where he had been convicted on a similar charge. He was brought to Chicago and on his testimony Lair was also convicted and imprisoned.

Marie has since married a man who wishes to protect her from the influence of her old life, but although not yet twenty years old and making an honest effort, what she has undergone has apparently so far warped and weakened her will that she is only partially successful in keeping her resolutions, and she sends each month to her parents in France ten or twelve dollars, which she confesses to have earned illicitly. It is as if the shameful experiences to which this little convent-bred Breton girl was forcibly subjected, had finally become registered in every fibre of her being until the forced demoralization has become genuine. She is as powerless now to save herself from her subjective temptations as she was helpless five years ago to save herself from her captors.

Such demoralization is, of course, most valuable to the white slave trader, for when a girl has become thoroughly accustomed to the life and testifies that she is in it of her own free will, she puts herself beyond the protection of the law. She belongs to a legally degraded class, without redress in courts of justice for personal outrages.

Marie, herself, at the end of her third year in America, wrote to the police appealing for help, but the lieutenant who in response to her letter visited the house, was convinced by Lair that she was there of her own volition and that therefore he could do nothing for her. It is easy to see why it thus becomes part of the business to break down a girl's moral nature by all those horrible devices which are constantly used by the owner of a white slave. Because life is so often shortened for these wretched girls, their owners degrade them morally as quickly as possible, lest death release them before their full profit has been secured. In addition to the quantity of sacrificed virtue, to the bulk of impotent suffering, which these white slaves represent, our civilization becomes permanently tainted with the vicious practices designed to accelerate the demoralization of unwilling victims in order to make them commercially valuable. Moreover, a girl thus rendered more useful to her owner, will thereafter fail to touch either the chivalry of men or the tenderness of women because good men and women have become convinced of her innate degeneracy, a word we have learned to use with the unction formerly placed upon original sin. The very revolt of society against such girls is used by their owners as a protection to the business.

The case against the captors of Marie, as well as twenty-four other cases, was ably and vigorously conducted by Edwin W. Sims, United

States District Attorney in Chicago. He prosecuted under a clause of the immigration act of 1908, which was unfortunately declared unconstitutional early the next year, when for the moment federal authorities found themselves unable to proceed directly against this international traffic. They could not act under the international white slave treaty signed by the contracting powers in Paris in 1904, and proclaimed by the President of the United States in 1908, because it was found impossible to carry out its provisions without federal police. The long consideration of this treaty by Congress made clear to the nation that it is in matters of this sort that navies are powerless and that as our international problems become more social, other agencies must be provided, a point which arbitration committees have long urged. The discussion of the international treaty brought the subject before the entire country as a matter for immediate legislation and for executive action, and the White Slave Traffic Act was finally passed by Congress in 1910, under which all later prosecutions have since been conducted. When the decision on the immigration clause rendered in 1909 threw the burden of prosecution back upon the states, Mr. Clifford Roe, then assistant State's Attorney, within one year investigated 348 such cases, domestic and foreign, and successfully prosecuted 91, carrying on the vigorous policy inaugurated by United States Attorney Sims. In 1908 Illinois passed the first pandering law in this country, changing the offence from disorderly conduct to a misdemeanor, and greatly increasing the penalty. In many states pandering is still so little defined as to make the crime merely a breach of manners and to put it in the same class of offences as selling a street-car transfer.

As a result of this vigorous action, Chicago became the first city to look the situation squarely in the face, and to make a determined businesslike fight against the procuring of girls. An office was established by public-spirited citizens where Mr. Roe was placed in charge and empowered to follow up the clues of the traffic wherever found and to bring the traffickers to justice; in consequence the white slave traders have become so frightened that the foreign importation of girls to Chicago has markedly declined. It is estimated by Mr. Roe that since 1909 about one thousand white slave traders, of whom thirty or forty were importers of foreign girls, have been driven away from the city.

Throughout the Congressional discussions of the white slave traffic, beginning with the Howell-Bennett Act in 1907, it was evident that the subject was closely allied to immigration, and when the immigration commission made a partial report to Congress in December, 1909, upon "the importation and harboring of women for immoral purposes, "their finding only emphasized the report of the Commissioner General of Immigration made earlier in the year. His report had traced the international traffic directly to New York, Chicago, Boston, Buffalo, New Orleans, Denver, Seattle, Portland, Salt Lake City, Ogden, and Butte. As the list of cities was comparatively small, it seemed not unreasonable to hope that the international traffic might be rigorously prosecuted, with the prospect of finally doing away with it in spite of its subtle methods, its multiplied ramifications, and its financial resources. Only officials of vigorous conscience can deal with this traffic; but certainly there can be no nobler service for federal and state officers to undertake than this protection of immigrant girls.

It is obvious that a foreign girl who speaks no English, who has not the remotest idea in what part of the city her fellow-countrymen live, who does not know the police station or any agency to which she may apply, is almost as valuable to a white slave trafficker as a girl imported directly for the trade. The trafficker makes every effort to intercept such a girl before she can communicate with her relations. Although great care is taken at Ellis Island, the girl's destination carefully indicated upon her ticket and her friends communicated with, after she boards the train the governmental protection is withdrawn and many untoward experiences may befall a girl between New York and her final destination. Only this year a Polish mother of the Hull-House neighborhood failed to find her daughter on a New York train upon which she had been notified to expect her, because the girl had been induced to leave the New York train at South Chicago, where she was met by two young men, one of them well known to the police, and the other a young Pole, purporting to have been sent by the girl's mother.

The immigrant girl also encounters dangers upon the very moment of her arrival. The cabmen and expressmen are often unscrupulous. One of the latter was recently indicted in Chicago upon the charge of regularly procuring immigrant girls for a disreputable hotel. The non-

English speaking girl handing her written address to a cabman has no means of knowing whither he will drive her, but is obliged to place herself implicitly in his hands. The Immigrants' Protective League has brought about many changes in this respect, but has upon its records some piteous tales of girls who were thus easily deceived.

An immigrant girl is occasionally exploited by her own lover whom she has come to America to marry. I recall the case of a Russian girl thus decoyed into a disreputable life by a man deceiving her through a fake marriage ceremony. Although not found until a year later, the girl had never ceased to be distressed and rebellious. Many Slovak and Polish girls, coming to America without their relatives, board in houses already filled with their countrymen who have also preceded their own families to the land of promise, hoping to earn money enough to send for them later. The immigrant girl is thus exposed to dangers at the very moment when she is least able to defend herself. Such a girl, already bewildered by the change from an old world village to an American city, is unfortunately sometimes convinced that the new country freedom does away with the necessity for a marriage ceremony. Many others are told that judgment for a moral lapse is less severe in America than in the old country. The last month's records of the Municipal Court in Chicago, set aside to hear domestic relation cases, show sixteen unfortunate girls, of whom eight were immigrant girls representing eight different nationalities. These discouraged and deserted girls become an easy prey for the procurers who have sometimes been in league with their lovers.

Even those girls who immigrate with their families and sustain an affectionate relation with them are yet often curiously free from chaperonage. The immigrant mothers do not know where their daughters work, save that it is in a vague "over there" or "down town." They themselves were guarded by careful mothers and they would gladly give the same oversight to their daughters, but the entire situation is so unlike that of their own peasant girlhoods that, discouraged by their inability to judge it, they make no attempt to understand their daughters' lives. The girls, realizing this inability on the part of their mothers, elated by that sense of independence which the first taste of self-support always brings, sheltered from observation during certain hours, are almost as free from social control as is the traditional young man who comes up from the country to take care of himself in a great city. These immigrant parents are, of course, quite unable to foresee that while a girl feels a certain restraint of public opinion from the tenement house neighbors among whom she lives, and while she also responds to the public opinion of her associates in a factory where she works, there is no public opinion at all operating as a restraint upon her in the hours which lie between the two, occupied in the coming and going to work through the streets of a city large enough to offer every opportunity for concealment. So much of the recreation which is provided by commercial agencies, even in its advertisements, deliberately plays upon the interest of sex because it is under such excitement and that of alcohol that money is most recklessly spent. The great human dynamic, which it has been the long effort of centuries to limit to family life, is deliberately utilized for advertising purposes, and it is inevitable that many girls yield to such allurements.

On the other hand, one is filled with admiration for the many immigrant girls who in the midst of insuperable difficulties resist all temptations. Such admiration was certainly due Olga, a tall, handsome girl, a little passive and slow, yet with that touch of dignity which a continued mood of introspection so often lends to the young. Olga had been in Chicago for a year living with an aunt who, when she returned to Sweden, placed her niece in a boarding-house which she knew to be thoroughly respectable. But a friendless girl of such striking beauty could not escape the machinations of those who profit by the sale of girls. Almost immediately Olga found herself beset by two young men who continually forced themselves upon her attention, although she refused all their invitations to shows and dances. In six months the frightened girl had changed her boarding-place four times, hoping that the men would not be able to follow her. She was also obliged constantly to look for a cheaper place, because the dull season in the cloak-making trade came early that year. In the fifth boarding-house she finally found herself so hopelessly in arrears that the landlady, tired of waiting for the "new cloak making to begin," at length fulfilled a long-promised threat, and one summer evening at nine o'clock literally put Olga into the street, retaining her trunk in payment of the debt. The girl walked the street for hours, until she fancied that she saw one of her persecutors in the distance, when she hastily took refuge in a sheltered doorway, crouching in terror. Although no one approached her, she sat there late into the night, apparently too apathetic to move. With the curious inconsequence of moody youth, she was not aroused to action by the situation in which she found herself. The incident epitomized to her the everlasting riddle of the universe to which she could see no solution and she drearily decided to throw herself into the lake. As she left the doorway at daybreak for this pitiful purpose, she attracted the attention of a passing policeman. In response to his questions, kindly at first but becoming exasperated as he was convinced that she was either "touched in her wits" or "guying" him, he obtained a confused story of the persecutions of the two young men, and in sheer bewilderment he finally took her to the station on the very charge against the thought of which she had so long contended.

The girl was doubtless sullen in court the next morning; she was resentful of the policeman's talk, she was oppressed and discouraged and therefore taciturn. She herself said afterwards that she "often got still that way." She so sharply felt the disgrace of arrest, after her long struggle for respectability, that she gave a false name and became involved in a story to which she could devote but half her attention, being still absorbed in an undercurrent of speculative thought which continually broke through the flimsy tale she was fabricating.

With the evidence before him, the judge felt obliged to sustain the policeman's charge, and as Olga could not pay the fine imposed, he sentenced her to the city prison. The girl, however, had appeared so strangely that the judge was uncomfortable and gave her in charge of a representative of the Juvenile Protective Association in the hope that she could discover the whole situation, meantime suspending the sentence. It took hours of patient conversation with the girl and the kindly services of a well-known alienist to break into her dangerous state of mind and to gain her confidence. Prolonged medical treatment averted the threatened melancholia and she was at last rescued from the meaningless despondency so hostile to life itself, which has claimed many young victims.

It is strange that we are so slow to learn that no one can safely live without companionship and affection, that the individual who tries the hazardous experiment of going without at least one of them is prone to be swamped by a black mood from within. It is as if we had to build little islands of affection in the vast sea of impersonal forces lest we be overwhelmed by them. Yet we know that in every large city there are hundreds of men whose business it is to discover girls thus hard pressed by loneliness and despair, to urge upon them the old excuse that "no one cares what you do," to fill them with cheap cynicism concerning the value of virtue, all to the end that a business profit may be secured.

Had Olga yielded to the solicitations of bad men and had the immigration authorities in the federal building of Chicago discovered her in the disreputable hotel in which her captors wanted to place her, she would have been deported to Sweden, sent home in disgrace from the country which had failed to protect her. Certainly the immigration laws might do better than to send a girl back to her parents, diseased and disgraced because America has failed to safeguard her virtue from the machinations of well-known but unrestrained criminals. The possibility of deportation on the charge of prostitution is sometimes utilized by jealous husbands or rejected lovers. Only last year a Russian girl came to Chicago to meet her lover and was deceived by a fake marriage. Although the man basely deserted her within a few weeks he became very jealous a year later when he discovered that she was about to be married to a prosperous fellow-countryman, and made charges against her to the federal authorities concerning her life in Russia. It was with the greatest difficulty that the girl was saved from deportation to Russia under circumstances which would have compelled her to take out a red ticket in Odessa, and to live forevermore the life with which her lover had wantonly charged her.

May we not hope that in time the nation's policy in regard to immigrants will become less negative and that a measure of protection will be extended to them during the three years when they are so liable to prompt deportation if they become criminals or paupers?

While it may be difficult for the federal authorities to accomplish this protection and will doubtless require an extension of the powers of the Department of Immigration, certainly no one will doubt that it is the business of the city itself to extend much more protection to young girls who so thoughtlessly walk upon its streets. Yet, in spite of the grave consequences which lack of proper supervision implies, the municipal treatment of commercialized vice not only differs in each city but varies greatly in the same city under changing administrations.

The situation is enormously complicated by the pharisaic attitude of the public which wishes to have the comfort of declaring the social evil to be illegal, while at the same time it expects the police department to regulate it and to make it as little obvious as possible. In reality the police, as they themselves know, are not expected to serve the public in this matter but to consult the desires of the politicians; for, next to the fast and loose police control of gambling, nothing affords better political material than the regulation of commercialized vice. First in line is the ward politician who keeps a disorderly saloon which serves both as a meeting-place for the vicious young men engaged in the traffic and as a market for their wares. Back of this the politician higher up receives his share of the toll which this business pays that it may remain undisturbed. The very existence of a segregated district under police regulation means, of course, that the existing law must be nullified or at least rendered totally inoperative. When police regulation takes the place of law enforcement a species of municipal blackmail inevitably becomes intrenched. The police are forced to regulate an illicit trade, but because the men engaged in an unlawful business expect to pay money for its protection, the corruption of the police department is firmly established and, as the Chicago vice commission report points out, is merely called "protection to the business." The practice of grafting thereafter becomes almost official. On the other hand, any man who attempts to show mercy to the victims of that business, or to regulate it from the victim's point of view, is considered a traitor to the cause. Quite recently a former inspector of police in Chicago established a requirement that every young girl who came to live in a disreputable house within a prescribed district must be reported to him within an hour after her arrival. Each one was closely questioned as to her reasons for entering into the life. If she was very young, she was warned of its inevitable consequences and urged to abandon her project. Every assistance was offered her to return to work and to live a normal life. Occasionally a girl was desperate and it was sometimes necessary that she be forcibly detained in the police station until her friends could be communicated with. More often she was glad to avail herself of the chance of escape; practically always, unless she had already become romantically entangled with a disreputable young man, whom she firmly believed to be her genuine lover and protector.

One day a telephone message came to Hull-House from the inspector asking us to take charge of a young girl who had been brought into the station by an older woman for registration. The girl's youth and the innocence of her replies to the usual questions convinced the inspector that she was ignorant of the life she was about to enter and that she probably believed she was simply registering her choice of a boarding-house. Her story which she told at Hull-House was as follows: She was a Milwaukee factory girl, the daughter of a Bohemian carpenter. Ten days before she had met a Chicago young man at a Milwaukee dance hall and after a brief courtship had promised to marry him, arranging to meet him in Chicago the following week. Fearing that her Bohemian mother would not approve of this plan, which she called "the American way of getting married," the girl had risen one morning even earlier than factory work necessitated and had taken the first train to Chicago. The young man met her at the station, took her to a saloon where he introduced her to a friend, an older woman, who, he said, would take good care of her. After the young man disappeared, ostensibly for the marriage license, the woman professed to be much shocked that the little bride had brought no luggage, and persuaded her that she must work a few weeks in order to earn money for her trousseau, and that she, an older woman who knew the city, would find a boarding-house and a place in a factory for her. She further induced her to write postal cards to six of her girl friends in Milwaukee, telling them of the kind lady in Chicago, of the good chances for work, and urging them to come down to the address which she sent. The woman told the unsuspecting girl that, first of all, a newcomer must register her place of residence with the police, as that was the law in Chicago. It was, of course, when the woman took her to the police station that the situation was disclosed. It needed but little investigation to make clear that the girl had narrowly escaped a well-organized plot and that the young man to whom she was engaged was an agent for a disreputable house. Mr. Clifford Roe took up the case with vigor, and although all efforts failed to find the young man, the woman who was his accomplice was fined one hundred and fifty dollars and costs.

The one impression which the trial left upon our minds was that all the men concerned in the prosecution felt a keen sense of outrage against the method employed to secure the girl, but took for granted that the life she was about to lead was in the established order of things, if she had chosen it voluntarily. In other words, if the efforts of the agent had gone far enough to involve her moral nature, the girl, who although unsophisticated, was twenty-one years old, could have remained, quite unchallenged, in the hideous life. The woman who was prosecuted was well known to the police and was fined, not for her daily occupation, but because she had become involved in interstate white slave traffic. One touch of nature redeemed the trial, for the girl suffered much more from the sense that she had been deserted by her lover than from horror over the fate she had escaped, and she was never wholly convinced that he had not been genuine. She asserted constantly, in order to account for his absence, that some accident must have befallen him. She felt that he was her natural protector in this strange Chicago to which she had come at his behest and continually resented any imputation of his motives. The betrayal of her confidence, the playing upon her natural desire for a home of her own, was a ghastly revelation that even when this hideous trade is managed upon the most carefully calculated commercial principles, it must still resort to the use of the oldest of the social instincts as its basis of procedure.

This Chicago police inspector, whose desire to protect young girls was so genuine and so successful, was afterward indicted by the grand jury and sent to the penitentiary on the charge of accepting "graft" from saloon-keepers and proprietors of the disreputable houses in his district. His experience was a dramatic and tragic portrayal of the position into which every city forces its police. When a girl who has been secured for the life is dissuaded from it, her rescue represents a definite monetary loss to the agency which has secured her and incurs the enmity of those who expected to profit by her. When this enmity has sufficiently accumulated, the active official is either "called down" by higher political authority, or brought to trial for those illegal practices which he shares with his fellow-officials. It is, therefore, easy to make such an inspector as ours suffer for his virtues, which are individual, by bringing charges against his grafting, which is general and almost official. So long as the customary prices for protection are adhered to, no one feels aggrieved; but the sentiment which prompts an inspector "to side with the girls" and to destroy thousands of dollars' worth of business is unjustifiable. He has not stuck to the rules of the game and the pack of enraged gamesters, under full cry of "morality," can very easily run him to ground, the public meantime being gratified that police corruption has been exposed and the offender punished. Yet hundreds of girls, who could have been discovered in no other way, were rescued by this man in his capacity of police inspector. On the other hand, he did little to bring to justice those responsible for securing the girls, and while he rescued the victim, he did not interfere with the source of supply. Had he been brought to trial for this indifference, it would have been impossible to find a grand jury to sustain the indictment. He was really brought to trial because he had broken the implied contract with the politicians; he had devised illicit and damaging methods to express that instinct for protecting youth and innocence, which every man on the police force doubtless possesses. Were this instinct freed from all political and extra legal control, it would in and of itself be a tremendous force against commercialized vice which is so dependent upon the exploitation of young girls. Yet the fortunes of the police are so tied up to those who profit by this trade and to their friends, the politicians, that the most well-meaning man upon the force is constantly handicapped. Several illustrations of this occur to me. Two years ago, when very untoward conditions were discovered in connection with a certain five-cent theatre, a young policeman arrested the proprietor, who was later brought before the grand jury, indicted and released upon bail for nine thousand dollars. The crime was a heinous one, involving the ruin of fourteen little girls; but so much political influence had been exerted on behalf of the proprietor, who was a relative of the republican committeeman of his ward, that although the license of the theatre was immediately revoked, it was reissued to his wife within a very few days and the man continued to be a menace to the community. When the young policeman who had made the arrest saw him in the neighborhood of the theatre talking to little girls and reported him, the officer was taken severely to task by the highest republican authority in the city. He was reprimanded for his activity and ordered transferred to the stockyards, eleven miles away. The policeman well understood that this was but the first step in the process called "breaking;" that after he had moved his family to the stockyards, in a few weeks he would be transferred elsewhere, and that this change of beat would be continued until he should at last be obliged to resign from the force. His offence, as he was plainly told, had been his ignorance of the fact that the theatre was under political protection. In short, the young officer had naively undertaken to serve the public without waiting for his instructions from the political bosses.

A flagrant example of the collusion of the police with vice is instanced by United States District Attorney Sims, who recently called upon the Chicago police to make twenty-four arrests on behalf of the United States government for violations of the white slave law, when all of the men liable to arrest left town two hours after the warrants were issued. To quote Mr. Sims: "We sent the secret service men who had been working in conjunction with the police back to Washington and brought in a fresh supply. These men did not work with the police, and within two weeks after the first set of secret service men had left Chicago, the men we wanted were back in town, and without the aid of the city police we arrested all of them."

When the legal control of commercialized vice is thus tied up with city politics the functions of the police become legislative, executive and judicial in regard to street solicitation: in a sense they also have power of license, for it lies with them to determine the number of women who are allowed to ply their trade upon the street. Some of these women are young earthlings, as it were, hoping to earn money for much-desired clothing or pleasure. Others are desperate creatures making one last effort before they enter a public hospital to face a miserable end; but by far the larger number are sent out under the protection of the men who profit by their earnings, or they are utilized to secure patronage for disreputable houses. The police regard the latter "as regular," and while no authoritative order is ever given, the patrolman understands that they are protected. On the other hand, "the straggler" is liable to be arrested by any officer who chooses, and she is subjected to a fine upon his unsupported word. In either case the police regard all such women as literally "abandoned," deprived of ordinary rights, obliged to live in specified residences, and liable to have their personal liberties invaded in a way that no other class of citizens would tolerate.

The recent establishment of the Night Court in New York registers an advance in regard to the treatment of these wretched women. Not only does the public gradually become cognizant of the treatment accorded them, but some attempt at discrimination is made between the first offenders and those hardened by long practice in that most hideous of occupations. Furthermore, an adult probation system is gradually being substituted for the system of fines which at present are levied in such wise as to virtually constitute a license and a partnership with the police department.

While American cities cannot be said to have adopted a policy either of suppression or one of regulation, because the police consider the former impracticable and the latter intolerable to public opinion, we may perhaps claim for America a little more humanity in its dealing with this class of women, a little less ruthlessness than that exhibited by the continental cities where reglementation is relentlessly assumed.

The suggestive presence of such women on the streets is perhaps one of the most demoralizing influences to be found in a large city, and such vigorous efforts as were recently made by a former chief of police in Chicago when he successfully cleared the streets of their presence, demonstrates that legal suppression is possible. At least this obvious temptation to young men and boys who are idly walking the streets might be avoided, for in an old formula one such woman "has cast down many wounded; yea, many strong men have been slain by her." Were the streets kept clear, many young girls would be spared familiar knowledge that such a method of earning money is open to them. I have personally known several instances in which young girls have begun street solicitation through sheer imitation. A young Polish woman found herself in dire straits after the death of her mother. Her only friends in America had moved to New York, she was in debt for her mother's funeral, and as it was the slack season of the miserable sweatshop sewing she had been doing, she was unable to find work. One evening when she was quite desperate with hunger, she stopped several men upon the street, as she had seen other girls do, and in her broken English asked them for something to eat. Only after a young man had given her a good meal at a restaurant did she realize the price she was expected to pay and the horrible things which the other girls were doing. Even in her shocked revolt she could not understand, of course, that she herself epitomized that hideous choice between starvation and vice which is perhaps the crowning disgrace of civilization.

The legal suppression of street solicitation would not only protect girls but would enormously minimize the risk and temptation to boys. The entire system of recruiting for commercialized vice is largely dependent upon boys who are scarcely less the victims of the system than are the girls themselves. Certainly this aspect of the situation must be seriously considered.

In 1908, when Mr. Clifford Roe conducted successful prosecutions against one hundred and fifty of these disreputable young men in Chicago, nearly all of them were local boys who had used their personal acquaintance to secure their victims. The accident of a long acquaintance with one of these boys, born in the Hull-House neighborhood, filled me with questionings as to how far society may be responsible for these wretched lads, many of them beginning a vicious career when they are but fifteen or sixteen years of age. Because the trade constantly demands very young girls, the procurers require the assistance of immature boys, for in this game above all others "youth calls to youth." Such a boy is often incited by the professional procurer to ruin a young girl, because the latter's position is much safer if the character of the girl is blackened before he sells her, and if he himself cannot be implicated in her downfall. He thus keeps himself within the letter of the law, and when he is even more cautious, he induces the boy to go through the ceremony of a legal marriage by promising him a percentage of his wife's first earnings.

Only yesterday I received a letter from a young man whom I had known from his early boyhood, written in the state penitentiary, where he is serving a life sentence. His father was a drunkard, but his mother was a fine woman, devoted to her children, and she had patiently supported her son Jim far beyond his school age. At the time of his trial, she pawned all her personal possessions and mortgaged her furniture in order to get three hundred dollars for his lawyer. Although Jim usually led the life of a loafer and had never supported his mother, he was affectionately devoted to her and always kindly and good-natured. Perhaps it was because he had been so long dependent upon a self-sacrificing woman that it became easy for him to be dependent upon his wife, a girl whom he met when he was temporarily acting as porter in a disreputable hotel. Through his long familiarity with vice, and the fact that many of his companions habitually lived upon the earnings of "their girls," he easily consented that his wife should continue her life, and he constantly accepted the money which she willingly gave him. After his marriage he still lived in his mother's house and refused to take more money from her, but she had no idea of the source of his income. One day he called at the hotel, as usual, to ask for his wife's earnings, and in a quarrel over the amount with the landlady of the house, he drew a revolver and killed her. Although the plea of self-defense was urged in the trial, his abominable manner of life so outraged both judge and jury that he received the maximum sentence. His mother still insists that he sincerely loved the girl, whom he so impulsively married and that he constantly tried to dissuade her from her evil life. Certain it is that Jim's wife and mother are both filled with genuine sorrow for his fate and that in some wise the educational and social resources in the city of his birth failed to protect him from his own lower impulses and from the evil companionship whose influence he could not withstand. He is but one of thousands of weak boys, who are constantly utilized to supply the white slave trafficker with young girls, for it has been estimated that at any given moment the majority of the girls utilized by the trade are under twenty years of age and that most of them were procured when younger. We cannot assume that the youths who are hired to entice and entrap these girls are all young fiends, degenerate from birth; the majority of them are merely out-of-work boys, idle upon the streets, who readily lend themselves to these base demands because nothing else is presented to them.

All the recent investigations have certainly made clear that the bulk of the entire traffic is conducted with the youth of the community, and that the social evil, ancient though it may be, must be renewed in our generation through its younger members. The knowledge of the youth of its victims doubtless in a measure accounts for the new sense of compunction which fills the community.

3

Amelioration of
Economic Conditions

◢ It may be possible to extract some small degree of comfort from the recent revelations of the white slave traffic when we reflect that at the present moment, in the midst of a freedom such as has never been accorded to young women in the history of the world, under an economic pressure grinding down upon the working girl at the very age when she most wistfully desires to be taken care of, it is necessary to organize a widespread commercial enterprise in order to procure a sufficient number of girls for the white slave market.

Certainly the larger freedom accorded to woman by our changing social customs and the phenomenal number of young girls who are utilized by modern industry, taken in connection with this lack of supply, would seem to show that the chastity of women is holding its own in that slow-growing civilization which ever demands more self-control and conscious direction on the part of the individuals sharing it.

Successive reports of the United States census indicate that self-supporting girls are increasing steadily in number each decade, until 59 per cent of all the young women in the nation between the ages of sixteen and twenty, are engaged in some gainful occupation. Year after year, as these figures increase, the public views them with complacency, almost with pride, and confidently depends upon the inner restraint and training of this girlish multitude to protect it from disaster. Nevertheless, the public is totally unable to determine at what moment these safeguards, evolved under former industrial conditions, may reach a breaking point, not because of economic freedom, but because of untoward economic conditions.

For the first time in history multitudes of women are laboring without the direct stimulus of family interest or affection, and they are also unable to proportion their hours of work and intervals of rest according to their strength; in addition to this for thousands of them the effort to obtain a livelihood fairly eclipses the very meaning of life itself. At the present moment no student of modern industrial conditions can possibly assert how far the superior chastity of woman, so rigidly maintained during the centuries, has been the result of her domestic surroundings, and certainly no one knows under what degree of economic pressure the old restraints may give way.

In addition to the monotony of work and the long hours, the small wages these girls receive have no relation to the standard of living which they are endeavoring to maintain. Discouraged and over-fatigued, they are often brought into sharp juxtaposition with the women who are obtaining much larger returns from their illicit trade. Society also ventures to capitalize a virtuous girl at much less than one who has yielded to temptation, and it may well hold itself responsible for the precarious position into which, year after year, a multitude of frail girls is placed.

The very valuable report recently issued by the vice commission of Chicago leaves no room for doubt upon this point. The report estimates the yearly profit of this nefarious business as conducted in Chicago to be between fifteen and sixteen millions of dollars. Although these enormous profits largely accrue to the men who conduct the business side of prostitution, the report emphasizes the fact that the average girl earns very much more in such a life than she can hope to earn by any honest work. It points out that the capitalized value of the average working girl is six thousand dollars, as she ordinarily earns six dollars a week, which is three hundred dollars a year, or five per cent on that sum. A girl who sells drinks in a disreputable saloon, earning in commissions for herself twenty-one dollars a week, is capitalized at a value of twenty-two thousand dollars. The report further estimates that the average girl who enters an illicit life under a protector or manager is able to earn twenty-five dollars a week, representing a capital of twenty-six thousand dollars. In other words, a girl in such a life "earns more than four times as much as she is worth as a factor in the social and industrial economy, where brains, intelligence, virtue and womanly charm should bring a premium." The argument is specious in that it does not record the economic value of the many later years in which the honest girl will live as wife and mother, in contrast to the premature death of the woman in the illicit trade, but the girl herself sees only the difference in the immediate earning possibilities in the two situations.

Nevertheless the supply of girls for the white slave traffic so far falls below the demand that large business enterprises have been developed throughout the world in order to secure a sufficient number of victims for this modern market. Over and over again in the criminal proceedings against the men engaged in this traffic, when questioned as to their motives, they have given the simple reply "that more girls are needed," and that they were "promised big money for them." Although economic pressure as a reason for entering an illicit life has thus been brought out in court by the evidence in a surprising number of cases, there is no doubt that it is often exaggerated; a girl always prefers to think that economic pressure is the reason for her downfall, even when the immediate causes have been her love of pleasure, her desire for finery, or the influence of evil companions. It is easy for her, as for all of us, to be deceived as to real motives. In addition to this the wretched girl who has entered upon an illicit life finds the experience so terrible that, day by day, she endeavors to justify herself with the excuse that the money she earns is needed for the support of some one dependent upon her, thus following habits established by generations of virtuous women who cared for feeble folk. I know one such girl living in a disreputable house in Chicago who has adopted a delicate child afflicted with curvature of the spine, whom she boards with respectable people and keeps for many weeks out of each year in an expensive sanitarium that it may receive medical treatment. The mother of the child, an inmate of the house in which the ardent foster-mother herself lives, is quite indifferent to the child's welfare and also rather amused at such solicitude. The girl has persevered in her course for five years, never however allowing the little invalid to come to the house in which she and the mother live. The same sort of devotion and self-sacrifice is often poured out upon the miserable man who in the beginning was responsible for the girl's entrance into the life and who constantly receives her earnings. She supports him in the luxurious life he may be living in another part of the town, takes an almost maternal pride in his good clothes and general prosperity, and regards him as the one person in all the world who understands her plight.

Most of the cases of economic responsibility, however, are not due to chivalric devotion, but arise from a desire to fulfill family obligations such as would be accepted by any conscientious girl. This was clearly revealed in conversations which were recently held with thirty-four girls, who were living at the same time in a rescue home, when twenty-two of them gave economic pressure as the reason for choosing the life which they had so recently abandoned. One piteous little widow of seventeen had been supporting her child and had been able to leave the life she had been leading only because her married sister offered to take care of the baby without the money formerly paid her. Another had been supporting her mother and only since her recent death was the girl sure that she could live honestly because she had only herself to care for.

The following story, fairly typical of the twenty-two involving economic reasons, is of a girl who had come to Chicago at the age of fifteen, from a small town in Indiana. Her father was too old to work and her mother was a dependent invalid. The brother who cared for the parents, with the help of the girl's own slender wages earned in the country store of the little town, became ill with rheumatism. In her desire to earn more money the country girl came to the nearest large city, Chicago, to work in a department store. The highest wage she could earn, even though she wore long dresses and called herself "experienced," was five dollars a week. This sum was of course inadequate even for her own needs and she was constantly filled with a corroding worry for "the folks at home." In a moment of panic, a fellow clerk who was "wise" showed her that it was possible to add to her wages by making appointments for money in the noon hour at down-town hotels. Having earned money in this way for a few months, the young girl made an arrangement with an older woman to be on call in the evenings whenever she was summoned by telephone, thus joining that large clandestine group of apparently respectable girls, most of whom yield to temptation only when hard pressed by debt incurred during illness or non-employment, or when they are facing some immediate necessity. This practice has become so general in the larger American cities as to be systematically conducted. It is perhaps the most sinister outcome of the economic pressure, unless one cites its corollary—the condition of thousands of young men whose low salaries so cruelly and unjustifiably postpone their marriages. For a long time the young saleswoman kept her position in the department store, retaining her honest wages for herself, but sending everything else to her family. At length however, she changed from her clandestine life to an openly professional one when she needed enough money to send her brother to Hot Springs, Arkansas, where she maintained him for a year. She explained that because he was now restored to health and able to support the family once more, she had left the life "forever and ever," expecting to return to her home in Indiana. She suspected that her brother knew of her experience, although she was sure that her parents did not, and she hoped that as she was not yet seventeen, she might be able to make a fresh start. Fortunately the poor child did not know how difficult that would be.

It is perhaps in the department store more than anywhere else that every possible weakness in a girl is detected and traded upon. For while it is true that "wherever many girls are gathered together more or less unprotected and embroiled in the struggle for a livelihood, near by will be hovering the procurers and evil-minded," no other place of employment is so easy of access as the department store. No visitor is received in a factory or office unless he has definite business there, whereas every purchaser is welcome at a department store, even a notorious woman well known to represent the demi-monde trade is treated with marked courtesy if she spends large sums of money. The primary danger lies in the fact that the comely saleswomen are thus easy of access. The disreputable young man constantly passes in and out, making small purchases from every pretty girl, opening an acquaintance with complimentary remarks; or the procuress, a fashionably-dressed woman, buys clothing in large amounts, sometimes for a young girl by her side, ostensibly her daughter. She condoles with the saleswoman upon her hard lot and lack of pleasure, and in the rôle of a kindly, prosperous matron invites her to come to her own home for a good time. The girl is sometimes subjected to temptation through the men and women in her own department, who tell her how invitations to dinners and theatres may be procured. It is not surprising that so many of these young, inexperienced girls are either deceived or yield to temptation in spite of the efforts made to protect them by the management and by the older women in the establishment.

The department store has brought together, as has never been done before in history, a bewildering mass of delicate and beautiful fabrics, jewelry and household decorations such as women covet, gathered skilfully from all parts of the world, and in the midst of this bulk of desirable possessions is placed an untrained girl with careful instructions as to her conduct for making sales, but with no guidance in regard to herself. Such a girl may be bitterly lonely, but she is expected to smile affably all day long upon a throng of changing customers. She may be without adequate clothing, although she stands in an emporium where it is piled about her, literally as high as her head. She may be faint for want of food but she may not sit down lest she assume "an attitude of inertia and indifference," which is against the rules. She may have a great desire for pretty things, but she must sell to other people at least twenty-five times the amount of her own salary, or she will not be retained. Because she is of the first generation of girls which has stood alone in the midst of trade, she is clinging and timid, and yet the only person, man or woman, in this commercial atmosphere who speaks to her of the care and protection which she craves, is seeking to betray her. Because she is young and feminine, her mind secretly dwells upon a future lover, upon a home, adorned with the most enticing of the household goods about her, upon a child dressed in the filmy fabrics she tenderly touches, and yet the only man who approaches her there acting upon the knowledge of this inner life of hers, does it with the direct intention of playing upon it in order to despoil her. Is it surprising that the average human nature of these young girls cannot, in many instances, endure this strain? Of fifteen thousand women employed in the down-town department stores of Chicago, the majority are Americans. We all know that the American girl has grown up in the belief that the world is hers from which to choose, that there is ordinarily no limit to her ambition or to her definition of success. She realizes that she is well mannered and well dressed and does not appear unlike most of her customers. She sees only one aspect of her countrywomen who come shopping, and she may well believe that the chief concern of life is fashionable clothing. Her interest and ambition almost inevitably become thoroughly worldly, and from the very fact that she is employed down-town, she obtains an exaggerated idea of the luxury of the illicit life all about her, which is barely concealed.

The fifth volume of the report of "Women and Child Wage Earners" in the United States gives the result of a careful inquiry into "the relation of wages to the moral condition of department store women." In connection with this, the investigators secured "the personal histories of one hundred immoral women," of whom ten were or had been employed in a department store. They found that while only one of the ten had been directly induced to leave the store for a disreputable life, six of them said that they had found "it was easier to earn money that way." The report states that the average employee in a department store earns about seven dollars a week, and that the average income of the one hundred immoral women covered by the personal histories, ranged from fifty dollars a week to one hundred dollars a week in exceptional cases. It is of these exceptional cases that the department store girl hears, and the knowledge becomes part of the unreality and glittering life that is all about her.

Another class of young women which is especially exposed to this alluring knowledge is the waitress in down-town cafés and restaurants. A recent investigation of girls in the segregated district of a neighboring city places waiting in restaurants and hotels as highest on the list of "previous occupations." Many waitresses are paid so little that they gratefully accept any fee which men may offer them. It is also the universal habit for customers to enter into easy conversation while being served. Some of them are lonely young men who have few opportunities to speak to women. The girl often quite innocently accepts an invitation for an evening, spent either in a theatre or dance hall, with no evil results, but this very lack of social convention exposes her to danger. Even when the proprietor means to protect the girls, a certain amount of familiarity must be borne, lest their resentment should diminish the patronage of the café. In certain restaurants, moreover, the waitresses doubtless suffer because the patrons compare them with the girls who ply their trade in disreputable saloons under the guise of serving drinks.

The following story would show that mere friendly propinquity may constitute a danger. Last summer an honest, straightforward girl from a small lake town in northern Michigan was working in a Chicago café, sending every week more than half of her wages of seven dollars to her mother and little sister, ill with tuberculosis, at home. The mother owned the little house in which she lived, but except for the vegetables she raised in her own garden and an occasional payment for plain sewing, she and her younger daughter were dependent upon the hard-working girl in Chicago. The girl's heart grew heavier week by week as the mother's letters reported that the sister was daily growing weaker. One hot day in August she received a letter from her mother telling her to come at once if she "would see sister before she died." At noon that day when sickened by the hot air of the café, and when the clatter of dishes, the buzz of conversation, the orders shouted through the slide seemed but a hideous accompaniment to her tormented thoughts, she was suddenly startled by hearing the name of her native town, and realized that one of her regular patrons was saying to her that he meant to take a night boat to M. at 8 o'clock and get out of this "infernal heat." Almost involuntarily she asked him if he would take her with him. Although the very next moment she became conscious what his consent implied, she did not reveal her fright, but merely stipulated that if she went with him he must agree to buy her a return ticket. She reached home twelve hours before her sister died, but when she returned to Chicago a week later burdened with the debt of an undertaker's bill, she realized that she had discovered a means of payment.

All girls who work down town are at a disadvantage as compared to factory girls, who are much less open to direct inducement and to the temptations which come through sheer imitation. Factory girls also have the protection of working among plain people who frankly designate an irregular life in harsh, old-fashioned terms. If a factory girl catches sight of the vicious life at all, she sees its miserable victims in all the wretchedness and sordidness of their trade in the poorer parts of the city. As she passes the opening doors of a disreputable saloon she may see for an instant three or four listless girls urging liquor upon men tired out with the long day's work and already sodden with drink. As she hurries along the street on a rainy night she may hear a sharp cry of pain from a sick-looking girl whose arm is being brutally wrenched by a rough man, and if she stops for a moment she catches his muttered threats in response to the girl's pleading "that it is too bad a night for street work." She sees a passing policeman shrug his shoulders as he crosses the street, and she vaguely knows that the sick girl has put herself beyond the protection of the law, and that the rough man has an understanding with the officer on the beat. She has been told that certain streets are "not respectable," but a furtive look down the length of one of them reveals only forlorn and ill-looking houses, from which all suggestion of homely domesticity has long since gone; a slovenly woman with hollow eyes and a careworn face holding up the lurching bulk of a drunken man is all she sees of its "denizens," although she may have known a neighbor's daughter who came home to die of a mysterious disease said to be the result of a "fast life," and whose disgraced mother "never again held up her head."

Yet in spite of all this corrective knowledge, the increasing nervous energy to which industrial processes daily accommodate themselves, and the speeding up constantly required of the operators, may at any moment so register their results upon the nervous system of a factory girl as to overcome her powers of resistance. Many a working girl at the end of a day is so hysterical and overwrought that her mental balance is plainly disturbed. Hundreds of working girls go directly to bed as soon as they have eaten their suppers. They are too tired to go from home for recreation, too tired to read and often too tired to sleep. A humane forewoman recently said to me as she glanced down the long room in which hundreds of young women, many of them with their shoes beside them, were standing: "I hate to think of all the aching feet on this floor; these girls all have trouble with their feet, some of them spend the entire evening bathing them in hot water." But aching feet are no more usual than aching backs and aching heads. The study of industrial diseases has only this year been begun by the federal authorities, and doubtless as more is known of the nervous and mental effect of over-fatigue, many moral breakdowns will be traced to this source. It is already easy to make the connection in definite cases: "I was too tired to care," "I was too tired to know what I was doing," "I was dead tired and sick of it all," "I was dog tired and just went with him," are phrases taken from the lips of reckless girls, who are endeavoring to explain the situation in which they find themselves.

Only slowly are laws being enacted to limit the hours of working women, yet the able brief presented to the United States supreme court on the constitutionality of the Oregon ten-hour law for women, based its plea upon the results of overwork as affecting women's health, the grave medical statement constantly broken into by a portrayal of the disastrous effects of overfatigue upon character. It is as yet difficult to distinguish between the results of long hours and the results of over-strain. Certainly the constant sense of haste is one of the most nerve-racking and exhausting tests to which the human system can be subjected. Those girls in the sewing industry whose mothers thread needles for them far into the night that they may sew without a moment's interruption during the next day; those girls who insert eyelets into shoes, for which they are paid two cents a case, each case containing twenty-four pairs of shoes, are striking victims of the over-speeding which is so characteristic of our entire factory system.

Girls working in factories and laundries are also open to the possibilities of accidents. The loss of only two fingers upon the right hand, or a broken wrist, may disqualify an operator from continuing in the only work in which she is skilled and make her struggle for respectability even more difficult. Varicose veins and broken arches in the feet are found in every occupation in which women are obliged to stand for hours, but at any moment either one may develop beyond purely painful symptoms into crippling incapacity. One such girl recently returning home after a long day's work deliberately sat down upon the floor of a crowded street car, explaining defiantly to the conductor and the bewildered passengers that "her feet would not hold out another minute." A young woman who only last summer broke her hand in a mangle was found in a rescue home in January, explaining her recent experience by the phrase that she was "up against it when leaving the hospital in October."

In spite of many such heart-breaking instances the movement for safeguarding machinery and securing indemnity for industrial accidents proceeds all too slowly. At a recent exhibition in Boston the knife of a miniature guillotine fell every ten seconds to indicate the rate of industrial accidents in the United States. Grisly as was the device, its hideousness might well have been increased had it been able to demonstrate the connection between certain of these accidents and the complete moral disaster which overtook their victims.

Yet factory girls who are subjected to this overstrain and overtime often find their greatest discouragement in the fact that after all their efforts they earn too little to support themselves. One girl said that she had first yielded to temptation when she had become utterly discouraged because she had tried in vain for seven months to save enough money for a pair of shoes. She habitually spent two dollars a week for her room, three dollars for her board, and sixty cents a week for car-fare, and she had found the forty cents remaining from her weekly wage of six dollars inadequate to do more than re-sole her old shoes twice. When the shoes became too worn to endure a third soling and she possessed but ninety cents towards a new pair, she gave up her strug-gle; to use her own contemptuous phrase, she "sold out for a pair of shoes."

Usually the phrases are less graphic, but after all they contain the same dreary meaning "Couldn't make both ends meet," "I had always been used to having nice things," "Couldn't make enough money to live on," "I got sick and ran behind," "Needed more money," "Impos-sible to feed and clothe myself," "Out of work, hadn't been able to save." Of course a girl in such a strait does not go out deliberately to find il-licit methods of earning money, she simply yields in a moment of ut-ter weariness and discouragement to the temptations she has been able to withstand up to that moment. The long hours, the lack of comforts, the low pay, the absence of recreation, the sense of "good times" all about her which she cannot share, the conviction that she is rapidly losing health and charm, rouse the molten forces within her. A swell-ing tide of self-pity suddenly storms the banks which have hitherto held her and finally overcomes her instincts for decency and righteousness, as well as the habit of clean living, established by generations of her forebears.

The aphorism that "morals fluctuate with trade" was long consid-ered cynical, but it has been demonstrated in Berlin, in London, in Ja-pan, as well as in several American cities, that there is a distinct increase in the number of registered prostitutes during periods of financial depression and even during the dull season of leading local industries. Out of my own experience I am ready to assert that very often all that is necessary to effectively help the girl who is on the edge of wrong-doing is to lend her money for her board until she finds work, provide the necessary clothing for which she is in such desperate need, persuade her relatives that she should have more money for her own expendi-tures, or find her another place at higher wages. Upon such simple eco-nomic needs does the tried virtue of a good girl sometimes depend.

Here again the immigrant girl is at a disadvantage. The average wage of two hundred newly arrived girls of various nationalities, Poles, Italians, Slovaks, Bohemians, Russians, Galatians, Croatians, Lithuanians, Roumanians, Germans, and Swedes, who were interviewed by the Immigrants' Protective League, was four dollars and a half a week for the first position which they had teen able to secure in Chicago. It often takes a girl several weeks to find her first place. During this period of looking for work the immigrant girl is subjected to great dangers. It is at such times that immigrants often exhibit symptoms of that type of disordered mind which alienists pronounce "due to conflict through poor adaptation." I have known several immigrant young men as well as girls who became deranged during the first year of life in America. A young Russian who came to Chicago in the hope of obtaining the freedom and self-development denied him at home, after three months of bitter disillusionment, with no work and insufficient food, was sent to the hospital for the insane. He only recovered after a group of his young countrymen devotedly went to see him each week with promises of work, the companionship at last establishing a sense of unbroken association. I also recall a Polish girl who became utterly distraught after weeks of sleeplessness and anxiety because she could not repay fifty dollars which she had borrowed from a countryman in Chicago for the purpose of bringing her sister to America. Her case was declared hopeless, but when the creditor made reassuring visits to the patient she began to mend and now, five years later, is not only free from debt, but has brought over the rest of the family, whose united earnings are slowly paying for a house and lot. Psychiatry is demonstrating the after-effects of fear upon the minds of children, but little has yet been done to show how far that fear of the future, arising from economic insecurity in the midst of new surroundings, has superinduced insanity among newly arrived immigrants. Such a state of nervous bewilderment and fright, added to that sense of expectation which youth always carries into new surroundings, often makes it easy to exploit the virtue of an immigrant girl. It goes without saying that she is almost always exploited industrially. A Russian girl recently took a place in a Chicago clothing factory at twenty cents a day, without in the least knowing that she was undercutting the wages of even that ill-paid industry. This girl rented a room for a dollar a week and all that she had to eat was given her by a friend in the same lodging house, who shared her own scanty fare with the newcomer.

In the clothing industry trade unionism has already established a minimum wage limit for thousands of women who are receiving the protection and discipline of trade organization and responding to the tonic of self-help. Low wages will doubtless in time be modified by Minimum Wage Boards representing the government's stake in industry, such as have been in successful operation for many years in certain British colonies and are now being instituted in England itself. As yet Massachusetts is the only state which has appointed a special commission to consider this establishment for America, although the Industrial Commission of Wisconsin is empowered to investigate wages and their effect upon the standard of living.

Anyone who has lived among working people has been surprised at the docility with which grown-up children give all of their earnings to their parents. This is, of course, especially true of the daughters. The fifth volume of the governmental report upon "Women and Child Wage Earners in the United States," quoted earlier, gives eighty-four per cent as the proportion of working girls who turn in all of their wages to the family fund. In most cases this is done voluntarily and cheerfully, but in many instances it is as if the tradition of woman's dependence upon her family for support held long after the actual fact had changed, or as if the tyranny established through generations when daughters could be starved into submission to a father's will, continued even after the rôles had changed, and the wages of the girl child supported a broken and dissolute father.

An over-restrained girl, from whom so much is exacted, will sometimes begin to deceive her family by failing to tell them when she has had a raise in her wages. She will habitually keep the extra amount for herself, as she will any overtime pay which she may receive. All such money is invariably spent upon her own clothing, which she, of course, cannot wear at home, but which gives her great satisfaction upon the streets.

The girl of the crowded tenements has no room in which to receive her friends or to read the books through which she shares the lives of assorted heroines, or, better still, dreams of them as of herself. Even if the living-room is not full of boarders or children or washing, it is comfortable neither for receiving friends nor for reading, and she finds upon the street her entire social field; the shop windows with their desirable garments hastily clothe her heroines as they travel the old roads of romance, the street cars rumbling noisily by suggest a delectable somewhere far away, and the young men who pass offer possibilities of the most delightful acquaintance. It is not astonishing that she insists upon clothing which conforms to the ideals of this all-absorbing street and that she will unhesitatingly deceive an uncomprehending family which does not recognize its importance.

One such girl had for two years earned money for clothing by filling regular appointments in a disreputable saloon between the hours of six and half-past seven in the evening. With this money earned almost daily she bought the clothes of her heart's desire, keeping them with the saloon-keeper's wife. She demurely returned to her family for supper in her shabby working clothes and presented her mother with her unopened pay envelope every Saturday night. She began this life at the age of fourteen after her Polish mother had beaten her because she had "elbowed" the sleeves and "cut out" the neck of her ungainly calico gown in a vain attempt to make it look "American." Her mother, who had so conscientiously punished a daughter who was "too crazy for clothes," could never of course comprehend how dangerous a combination is the girl with an unsatisfied love for finery and the opportunities for illicit earning afforded on the street. Yet many sad cases may be traced to such lack of comprehension. Charles Booth states that in England a large proportion of parents belonging to the working and even lower middle classes, are unacquainted with the nature of the lives led by their own daughters, a result doubtless of the early freedom of the street accorded city children. Too often the mothers themselves are totally ignorant of covert dangers. A few days ago I held in my hand a pathetic little pile of letters written by a desperate young girl of fifteen before she attempted to commit suicide. These letters were addressed to her lover, her girl friends, and to the head of the rescue home, but none to her mother towards whom she felt a bitter resentment "because she did not warn me." The poor mother after the death of her husband had gone to live with a married daughter, but as the son-in-law would not "take in two" she had told the youngest daughter, who had already worked for a year as an apprentice in a dressmaking establishment, that she must find a place to live with one of her girl friends. The poor child had found this impossible, and three days after the breaking up of her home she had fallen a victim to a white slave trafficker, who had treated her most cruelly and subjected her to unspeakable indignities. It was only when her "protector" left the city, frightened by the unwonted activity of the police, due to a wave of reform, that she found her way to the rescue home, and in less than five months after the death of her father she had purchased carbolic acid and deliberately "courted death for the nameless child" and herself.

Another experience during which a girl faces a peculiar danger is when she has lost one "job" and is looking for another. Naturally she loses her place in the slack season and pursues her search at the very moment when positions are hardest to find, and her unemployment is therefore most prolonged. Perhaps nothing in our social order is so unorganized and inchoate as our method, or rather lack of method, of placing young people in industry. This is obvious from the point of view of their first positions when they leave school at the unstable age of four-teen, or from the innumerable places they hold later, often as high as ten a year, when they are dismissed or change voluntarily through sheer restlessness. Here again a girl's difficulty is often increased by the lack of sympathy and understanding on the part of her parents. A girl is of-ten afraid to say that she has lost her place and pretends to go to work each morning while she is looking for a new one; she postpones telling them at home day by day, growing more frantic as the usual pay-day approaches. Some girls borrow from loan sharks in order to take the customary wages to their parents, others fall victims to unscrupulous employment agencies in their eagerness to take the first thing offered.

The majority of these girls answer the advertisements in the daily papers as affording the cheapest and safest way to secure a position. These out-of-work girls are found, sometimes as many as forty or fifty at a time, in the rest rooms of the department stores, waiting for the new edition of the newspapers after they have been the rounds of the morning advertisements and have found nothing.

Of course such a possible field as these rest rooms is not overlooked by the procurer, who finds it very easy to establish friendly relations through the offer of the latest edition of the newspaper. Even pennies are precious to a girl out of work and she is also easily grateful to anyone who expresses an interest in her plight and tells her of a position. Two representatives of the Juvenile Protective Association of Chicago, during a period of three weeks, arrested and convicted seventeen men and three women who were plying their trades in the rest rooms of nine department stores. The managers were greatly concerned over this exposure and immediately arranged both for more intelligent matrons and greater vigilance. One of the less scrupulous stores voluntarily gave up a method of advertising carried on in the rest room itself where a demonstrator from "the beauty counter" made up the faces of the patrons of the rest room with the powder and paint procurable in her department below. The out-of-work girls especially availed themselves of this privilege and hoped that their search would be easier when their pale, woe-begone faces were "made beautiful." The poor girls could not know that a face thus made up enormously increased their risks.

A number of girls also came early in the morning as soon as the rest rooms were open. They washed their faces and arranged their hair and then settled to sleep in the largest and easiest chairs the room afforded. Some of these were out-of-work girls also determined to take home their wages at the end of the week, each pretending to her mother that she had spent the night with a girl friend and was working all day as usual. How much of this deception is due to parental tyranny and how much to a sense of responsibility for younger children or invalids, it is impossible to estimate until the number of such recorded cases is much larger. Certain it is that the long habit of obedience, as well as the feeling of family obligation established from childhood, is often utilized by the white slave trafficker.

Difficult as is the position of the girl out of work when her family is exigent and uncomprehending, she has incomparably more protection than the girl who is living in the city without home ties. Such girls form sixteen per cent of the working women of Chicago. With absolutely every penny of their meagre wages consumed in their inadequate living, they are totally unable to save money. That loneliness and detachment which the city tends to breed in its inhabitants is easily intensified in such a girl into isolation and a desolating feeling of belonging nowhere. All youth resents the sense of the enormity of the universe in relation to the insignificance of the individual life, and youth, with that intense self-consciousness which makes each young person the very centre of all emotional experience, broods over this as no older person can possibly do. At such moments a black oppression, the instinctive fear of solitude, will send a lonely girl restlessly to walk the streets even when she is "too tired to stand," and when her desire for companionship in itself constitutes a grave danger. Such a girl living in a rented room is usually without any place in which to properly receive callers. An investigation was recently made in Kansas City of 411 lodging-houses in which young girls were living; less than 30 per cent were found with a parlor in which guests might be received. Many girls quite innocently permit young men to call upon them in their bedrooms, pitifully disguised as "sitting-rooms," but the danger is obvious, and the standards of the girl gradually become lowered.

Certainly during the trying times when a girl is out of work she should have much more intelligent help than is at present extended to her; she should be able to avail herself of the state employment agencies much more than is now possible, and the work of the newly established vocational bureaus should be enormously extended.

When once we are in earnest about the abolition of the social evil, society will find that it must study industry from the point of view of the producer in a sense which has never been done before. Such a study with reference to industrial legislation will ally itself on one hand with the trades-union movement, which insists upon a living wage and shorter hours for the workers, and also upon an opportunity for self-direction, and on the other hand with the efficiency movement, which would refrain from over-fatiguing an operator as it would from over-speeding a machine. In addition to legislative enactment and the historic trade-union effort, the feebler and newer movement on the part of the employers is being reinforced by the welfare secretary, who is not only devising recreational and educational plans, but is placing before the employer much disturbing information upon the cost of living in relation to the pitiful wages of working girls. Certainly employers are growing ashamed to use the worn-out, hypocritical pretence of employing only the girl "protected by home influences" as a device for reducing wages. Help may also come from the consumers, for an increasing number of them, with compunctions in regard to tempted young employees, are not only unwilling to purchase from the employer who underpays his girls and thus to share his guilt, but are striving in divers ways to modify existing conditions.

As working women enter fresh fields of labor which ever open up anew as the old fields are submerged behind them, society must endeavor to speedily protect them by an amelioration of the economic conditions which are now so unnecessarily harsh and dangerous to health and morals. The world-wide movement for establishing governmental control of industrial conditions is especially concerned for working women. Fourteen of the European countries prohibit all night work for women and almost every civilized country in the world is considering the number of hours and the character of work in which women may be permitted to safely engage.

Although amelioration comes about so slowly that many young girls are sacrificed each year under conditions which could so easily and reasonably be changed, nevertheless it is apparently better to overcome the dangers in this new and freer life, which modern industry has opened to women, than it is to attempt to retreat into the domestic industry of the past; for all statistics of prostitution give the largest number of recruits for this life as coming from domestic service and the second largest number from girls who live at home with no definite occupation whatever. Therefore, although in the economic aspect of the social evil more than in any other, do we find ground for despair, at the same time we discern, as nowhere else, the young girl's stubborn power of resistance. Nevertheless, the most superficial survey of her surroundings shows the necessity for ameliorating, as rapidly as possible, the harsh economic conditions which now environ her.

That steadily increasing function of the state by which it seeks to protect its workers from their own weakness and degradation, and insists that the livelihood of the manual laborer shall not be beaten down below the level of efficient citizenship, assumes new forms almost daily. From the human as well as the economic standpoint there is an obligation resting upon the state to discover how many victims of the white slave traffic are the result of social neglect, remedial incapacity, and the lack of industrial safeguards, and how far discontinuous employment and non-employment are factors in the breeding of discouragement and despair.

Is it because our modern industrialism is so new that we have been

slow to connect it with the poverty and vice all about us? The socialists talk constantly of the relation of economic law to destitution and
point out the connection between industrial maladjustment and individual wrongdoing, but certainly the study of social conditions, the
obligation to eradicate vice, cannot belong to one political party or to
one economic school. It must be recognized as a solemn obligation of
existing governments, and society must realize that economic conditions can only be made more righteous and more human by the un-
ceasing devotion of generations of men.

4

Moral Education
and Legal Protection
of Children

No great wrong has ever arisen more clearly to the social consciousness of a generation than has that of commercialized vice in the consciousness of ours, and that we are so slow to act is simply another evidence that human nature has a curious power of callous indifference towards evils which have been so entrenched that they seem part of that which has always been. Educators of course share this attitude; at moments they seem to intensify it, although at last an educational movement in the direction of sex hygiene is beginning in the schools and colleges. Primary schools strive to satisfy the child's first questionings regarding the beginnings of human life and approach the subject through simple biological instruction which at least places this knowledge on a par with other natural facts. Such teaching is an enormous advance for the children whose curiosity would otherwise have been satisfied from poisonous sources and who would have learned of simple physiological matters from such secret undercurrents of corrupt knowledge as to have forever perverted their minds. Yet this first direct step towards an adequate educational approach to this subject has been surprisingly difficult owing to the self-consciousness of grown-up people; for while the children receive the teaching quite simply, their parents often take alarm. Doubtless cooperation with parents will be necessary before the subject can fall into its proper place in the schools. In Chicago, the largest women's club in the city has established normal courses in sex hygiene attended both by teachers and mothers, the National and State Federations of Women's Clubs are gradually preparing thousands of women throughout America for fuller co-operation with the schools in this difficult matter. In this, as in so many other educational movements, Germany has led the way. Two publications are issued monthly in Berlin, which promote not only more effective legislation but more adequate instruction in the schools on this basic subject. These journals are supported by men and women anxious for light for the sake of their children. Some of them were first stirred to action by Wedekind's powerful drama "The Awakening of Spring," which, with Teutonic grimness, thrusts over the footlights the lesson that death and degradation may be the fate of a group of gifted school-children, because of the cowardly reticence of their parents.

A year ago the Bishop of London gathered together a number of influential people and laid before them his convictions that the root of the social evil lay in so-called "parental modesty," and that in the quickening of the parental conscience lay the hope for the "lifting up of England's moral tone which has for so long been the despair of England's foremost men."

In America the eighth year-book of the National Society for the Scientific Study of Education treats of this important subject with great ability, massing the agencies and methods in impressive array. Many other educational journals and organized societies could be cited as expressing a new conscience in regard to this world-old evil. The expert educational opinion which they represent is practically agreed that for older children the instruction should not be confined to biology and hygiene, but may come quite naturally in history and literature, which record and portray the havoc wrought by the sexual instinct when uncontrolled, and also show that, when directed and spiritualized, it has become an inspiration to the loftiest devotions and sacrifices. The youth thus taught sees this primal instinct not only as an essential to the continuance of the race, but also, when it is transmuted to the highest ends, as a fundamental factor in social progress. The entire subject is broadened out in his mind as he learns that his own struggle is a common experience. He is able to make his own interpretations and to combat the crude inferences of his patronizing companions. After all, no young person will be able to control his impulses and to save himself from the grosser temptations, unless he has been put under the sway of nobler influences. Perhaps we have yet to learn that the inhibitions of character as well as its reinforcements come most readily through idealistic motives.

Certainly all the great religions of the world have recognized youth's need of spiritual help during the trying years of adolescence. The ceremonies of the earliest religions deal with this instinct almost to the exclusion of others, and all later religions attempt to provide the youth with shadowy weapons for the struggle which lies ahead of him, for the wise men in every age have known that only the power of the spirit can overcome the lusts of the flesh. In spite of this educational advance, courses of study in many public and private schools are still prepared exactly as if educators had never known that at fifteen or sixteen years of age, the will power being still weak, the bodily desires are keen and insistent. The head master of Eton, Mr. Lyttleton, who has given much thought to this gap in the education of youth says, "The certain result of leaving an enormous majority of boys unguided and uninstructed in a matter where their strongest passions are concerned, is that they grow up to judge of all questions connected with it, from a purely selfish point of view." He contends that this selfishness is due to the fact that any single suggestion or hint which boys receive on the subject comes from other boys or young men who are under the same potent influences of ignorance, curiosity and the claims of self. No wholesome counter-balance of knowledge is given, no attempt is made to invest the subject with dignity or to place it in relation to the welfare of others and to universal law. Mr. Lyttleton contends that this alone can explain the peculiarly brutal attitude towards "outcast" women which is a sustained cruelty to be discerned in no other relation of English life. To quote him again: "But when the victims of man's cruelty are not birds or beasts but our own countrywomen, doomed by the hundred thousand to a life of unutterable shame and hopeless misery, then and then only the general average tone of young men becomes hard and brutally callous or frivolous with a kind of coarse frivolity not exhibited in relation to any other form of human suffering." At the present moment thousands of young people in our great cities possess no other knowledge of this grave social evil which may at any moment become a dangerous personal menace, save what is imparted to them in this brutal flippant spirit. It has been said that the child growing up in the midst of civilization receives from its parents and teachers something of the accumulated experience of the world on all other subjects save upon that of sex. On this one subject alone each generation learns little from its predecessors.

An educator has lately pointed out that it is an old lure of vice to pretend that it alone deals with manliness and reality, and he complains that it is always difficult to convince youth that the higher planes of life contain anything but chilly sentiments. He contends that young people are therefore prone to receive moralizing and admonitions with polite attention, but when it comes to action, they carefully observe the life about them in order to conduct themselves in such wise as to be part of the really desirable world inhabited by men of affairs. Owing to this attitude, many young people living in our cities at the present moment have failed to apprehend the admonitions of religion and have never responded to its inner control. It is as if the impact of the world had stunned their spiritual natures, and as if this had occurred at the very time that a most dangerous experiment is being tried. The public gaieties formerly allowed in Catholic countries where young people were restrained by the confessional, are now permitted in cities where this restraint is altogether unknown to thousands of young people, and only faintly and traditionally operative upon thousands of others. The puritanical history of American cities assumes that these gaieties are forbidden, and that the streets are sober and decorous for conscientious young men and women who need no external protection. This ungrounded assumption, united to the fact that no adult has the confidence of these young people, who are constantly subjected to a multitude of imaginative impressions, is almost certain to result disastrously.

The social relationships in a modern city are so hastily made and often so superficial, that the old human restraints of public opinion, long sustained in smaller communities, have also broken down. Thousands of young men and women in every great city have received none of the lessons in self-control which even savage tribes imparted to their children when they taught them to master their appetites as well as their emotions. These young people are perhaps further from all community restraint and genuine social control than the youth of the community have ever been in the long history of civilization. Certainly only the modern city has offered at one and the same time every possible stimulation for the lower nature and every opportunity for secret vice. Educators apparently forget that this unrestrained stimulation of young people, so characteristic of our cities, although developing very rapidly, is of recent origin, and that we have not yet seen the outcome. The present education of the average young man has given him only the most unreal protection against the temptations of the city. Schoolboys are subjected to many lures from without just at the moment when they are filled with an inner tumult which utterly bewilders them and concerning which no one has instructed them save in terms of empty precept and unintelligible warning.

We are authoritatively told that the physical difficulties are enormously increased by uncontrolled or perverted imaginations, and all sound advice to young men in regard to this subject emphasizes a clean mind, exhorts an imagination kept free from sensuality and insists upon days filled with wholesome athletic interests. We allow this régime to be exactly reversed for thousands of young people living in the most crowded and most unwholesome parts of the city. Not only does the stage in its advertisements exhibit all the allurements of sex to such an extent that a play without a "love interest" is considered foredoomed to failure, but the novels which form the sole reading of thousands of young men and girls deal only with the course of true or simulated love, resulting in a rose-colored marriage, or in variegated misfortunes.

Often the only recreation possible for young men and young women together is dancing, in which it is always easy to transgress the proprieties. In many public dance halls, however, improprieties are deliberately fostered. The waltzes and two-steps are purposely slow, the couples leaning heavily on each other barely move across the floor, all the jollity and bracing exercise of the peasant dance is eliminated, as is all the careful decorum of the formal dance. The efforts to obtain pleasure or to feed the imagination are thus converged upon the senses which it is already difficult for young people to understand and to control. It is therefore not remarkable that in certain parts of the city groups of idle young men are found whose evil imaginations have actually inhibited their power for normal living. On the streets or in the poolrooms where they congregate their conversation, their tales of adventure, their remarks upon women who pass by, all reveal that they have been caught in the toils of an instinct so powerful and primal that when left without direction it can easily overwhelm its possessor and swamp his faculties. These young men, who do no regular work, who expect to be supported by their mothers and sisters and to get money for the shows and theatres by any sort of disreputable undertaking, are in excellent training for the life of the procurer, and it is from such groups that they are recruited. There is almost a system of apprenticeship, for boys when very small act as "look-outs" and are later utilized to make acquaintances with girls in order to introduce them to professionals. From this they gradually learn the method of procuring girls and at last do an independent business. If one boy is successful in such a life, throughout his acquaintance runs the rumor that a girl is an asset that will bring a larger return than can possibly be earned in hardworking ways. Could the imaginations of these young men have been controlled and cultivated, could the desire for adventure have been directed into wholesome channels, could these idle boys have been taught that, so far from being manly they were losing all virility, could higher interests have been aroused and standards given them in relation to this one aspect of life, the entire situation of commercialized vice would be a different thing.

The girls with a desire for adventure seem confined to this one dubious outlet even more than the boys, although there are only one-eighth as many delinquent girls as boys brought into the juvenile court in Chicago, the charge against the girls in almost every instance involves a loss of chastity. One of them who was vainly endeavoring to formulate the causes of her downfall, concentrated them all in the single statement that she wanted the other girls to know that she too was a "good Indian." Such a girl, while she is not an actual member of a gang of boys, is often attached to one by so many loyalties and friendships that she will seldom testify against a member, even when she has been injured by him. She also depends upon the gang when she requires bail in the police court or the protection that comes from political influence, and she is often very proud of her quasi-membership. The little girls brought into the juvenile court are usually daughters of those poorest immigrant families living in the worst type of city tenements, who are frequently forced to take boarders in order to pay the rent. A surprising number of little girls have first become involved in wrongdoing through the men of their own households. A recent inquiry among 130 girls living in a sordid red light district disclosed the fact that a majority of them had thus been victimized and the wrong had come to them so early that they had been despoiled at an average age of eight years. Looking upon the forlorn little creatures, who are often brought into the Chicago juvenile court to testify against their own relatives, one is seized with that curious compunction Goethe expressed in the now hackneyed line from "Mignon:"

"Was hat Man dir, du armes Kind, gethan?"

One is also inclined to reproach educators for neglecting to give children instruction in play when one sees the unregulated amusement parks which are apparently so dangerous to little girls twelve or fourteen years old. Because they are childishly eager for amusement and totally unable to pay for a ride on the scenic railway or for a ticket to an entertainment, these disappointed children easily accept many favors from the young men who are standing near the entrances for the express purpose of ruining them. The hideous reward which is demanded from them later in the evening, after they have enjoyed the many "treats " which the amusement park offers, apparently seems of little moment. Their childish minds are filled with the memory of the lurid pleasures to the oblivion of the later experience, and they eagerly tell their companions of this possibility "of getting in to all the shows." These poor little girls pass unnoticed amidst a crowd of honest people seeking recreation after a long day's work, groups of older girls walking and talking gaily with young men of their acquaintance, and happy children holding their parents' hands. This cruel exploitation of the childish eagerness for pleasure is, of course, possible only among a certain type of forlorn city children who are totally without standards and into whose colorless lives a visit to the amusement park brings the acme of delirious excitement. It is possible that these children are the inevitable product of city life; in Paris, little girls at local fêtes wishing to ride on the hobby horse frequently buy the privilege at a fearful price from the man directing the machinery, and a physician connected with the New York Society for the Prevention of Cruelty to Children writes: "It is horribly pathetic to learn how far a nickel or a quarter will go towards purchasing the virtue of these children"

The home environment of such children has been similar to that of many others who come to grief through the five-cent theatres. These eager little people, to whom life has offered few pleasures, crowd around the door hoping to be taken in by some kind soul and, when they have been disappointed over and over again and the last performance is about to begin, a little girl may be induced unthinkingly to barter her chastity for an entrance fee.

Many children are also found who have been decoyed into their first wrong-doing through the temptation of the saloon, in spite of the fact that one of the earliest regulations in American cities for the protection of children was the prohibition of the sale of liquor to minors. That children may be easily demoralized by the influence of a disorderly saloon was demonstrated recently in Chicago; one of these saloons was so situated that the pupils of a public school were obliged to pass it and from the windows of the schoolhouse itself could see much of what was passing within the place. An effort was made by the Juvenile Protective Association to have it closed by the chief of police, but although he did so, it was opened again the following day. The Association then took up the matter with the mayor, who refused to interfere, insisting that the objectionable features had been eliminated. Through months of effort, during which time the practices of the place remained quite unchanged, one group after another of public-spirited citizens endeavored to suppress what had become a public scandal, only to find that the place was protected by brewery interests which were more powerful, both financially and politically, than themselves. At last, after a peculiarly flagrant case involving a little girl, the mothers of the neighborhood arranged a mass meeting in the schoolhouse itself, inviting local officials to be present. The mothers then produced a mass of testimony which demonstrated that dozens and hundreds of children had been directly or indirectly affected by the place whose removal they demanded. A meeting so full of genuine anxiety and righteous indignation could not well be disregarded, and the compulsory education department was at last able to obtain a revocation of the license. The many people who had so long tried to do away with this avowedly disreputable saloon received a fresh impression of the menace to children who became sophisticated by daily familiarity with vice. Yet many mothers, hard pressed by poverty, are obliged to rent houses next to vicious neighborhoods and their children very early become familiar with all the outer aspects of vice. Among them are the children of widows who make friends with their dubious neighbors during the long days while their mothers are at work. I recall two sisters in one family whose mother had moved her household to the borders of a Chicago segregated district, apparently without knowing the character of the neighborhood. The little sisters, twelve and eight years old, accepted many invitations from a kind neighbor to come into her house to see her pretty things. The older girl was delighted to be "made up" with powder and paint and to try on long dresses, while the little one who sang very prettily was taught some new songs, happily without understanding their import. The tired mother knew nothing of what the children did during her absence, until an honest neighbor who had seen the little girls going in and out of the district, interfered on their behalf. The frightened mother moved back to her old neighborhood which she had left in search of cheaper rent, her pious soul stirred to its depths that the children for whom she patiently worked day by day had so narrowly escaped destruction.

Who cannot recall at least one of these desperate mothers, overworked and harried through a long day, prolonged by the family washing and cooking into the evening, followed by a night of foreboding and misgiving because the very children for whom her life is sacrificed are slowly slipping away from her control and affection? Such a spectacle forces one into an agreement with Wells, that it is a "monstrous absurdity" that women who are "discharging their supreme social function, that of rearing children, should do it in their spare time, as it were, while they 'earn their living' by contributing some half-mechanical element to some trivial industrial product." Nevertheless, such a woman whose wages are fixed on the basis of individual subsistence, who is quite unable to earn a family wage, is still held by a legal obligation to support her children with the desperate penalty of forfeiture if she fail.

I can recall a very intelligent woman who long brought her children to the Hull-House day nursery with this result at the end of ten years of devotion: the little girl is almost totally deaf owing to neglect following a case of measles, because her mother could not stop work in order to care for her; the youngest boy has lost a leg flipping cars; the oldest boy has twice been arrested for petty larceny; the twin boys, in spite of prolonged sojourns in the parental school, have been such habitual truants that their natural intelligence has secured little aid from education. Of the five children three are now in semi-penal institutions, supported by the state. It would not therefore have been so uneconomical to have boarded them with their own mother, requiring a standard of nutrition and school attendance at least up to that national standard of nurture which the more advanced European governments are establishing.

The recent Illinois law, providing that the children of widows may be supported by public funds paid to the mother upon order of the juvenile court, will eventually restore a mother's care to these poor children; but in the meantime, even the poor mother who is receiving such aid, in her forced search for cheap rent maybe continually led nearer to the notoriously evil districts. Many appeals made to landlords of disreputable houses in Chicago on behalf, of the children living adjacent to such property have never secured a favorable response. It is apparently difficult for the average property owner to resist the high rents which houses in certain districts of the city can command if rented for purposes of vice. I recall two small frame houses identical in type and value standing side by side. One which belonged to a citizen without scruples was rented for $30.00 a month, the other belonging to a conscientious man was rented for $9.00 a month. The supposedly respectable landlords defend themselves behind the old sophistry: "If I did not rent my house for such a purpose, someone else would," and the more hardened ones say that "It is all in the line of business." Both of them are enormously helped by the secrecy surrounding the ownership of such houses, although it is hoped that the laws requiring the name of the owner and the agent of every multiple house to be posted in the public hallway will at length break through this protection, and the discovered Landlords will then be obliged to pay the fine to which the law specifically states they have made themselves liable. In the meantime, women forced to find cheap rents are subjected to one more handicap in addition to the many others poverty places upon them. Such experiences may explain the fact that English figures show a very large proportion of widows and deserted women among the prostitutes in those large towns which maintain segregated districts.

The deprivation of a mother's care is most frequently experienced by the children of the poorest colored families who are often forced to live in disreputable neighborhoods because they literally cannot rent houses anywhere else. Both because rents are always high for colored people and because the colored mothers are obliged to support their children, seven times as many of them, in proportion to their entire number, as of the white mothers, the actual number of colored children neglected in the midst of temptation is abnormally large. So closely is child life founded upon the imitation of what it sees that the child who knows all evil is almost sure in the end to share it. Colored children seldom roam far from their own neighborhoods: in the public playgrounds, which are theoretically open to them, they are made so uncomfortable by the slights of other children that they learn to stay away, and, shut out from legitimate recreation, are all the more tempted by the careless, luxurious life of a vicious neighborhood. In addition to the colored girls who have thus from childhood grown familiar with the outer aspects of vice, are others who are sent into the district in the capacity of domestic servants by unscrupulous employment agencies who would not venture to thus treat a white girl. The community forces the very people who have confessedly the shortest history of social restraint, into a dangerous proximity with the vice districts of the city. This results, as might easily be predicted, in a very large number of colored girls entering a disreputable life. The negroes themselves believe that the basic cause for the high percentage of colored prostitutes is the recent enslavement of their race with its attendant unstable marriage and parental status, and point to thousands of slave sales that but two generations ago disrupted the negroes' attempts at family life. Knowing this as we do, it seems all the more unjustifiable that the nation which is responsible for the broken foundations of this family life should carelessly permit the negroes, making their first struggle towards a higher standard of domesticity, to be subjected to the most flagrant temptations which our civilization tolerates.

The imaginations of even very young children may easily be forced into sensual channels. A little girl, twelve years old, was one day brought to the psychopathic clinic connected with the Chicago juvenile court. She had been detained under police surveillance for more than a week, while baffled detectives had in vain tried to verify the statements she had made to her Sunday-school teacher in great detail of certain horrible experiences which had befallen her. For at least a week no one concerned had the remotest idea that the child was fabricating. The police thought that she had merely grown confused as to the places to which she had been "carried unconscious." The mother gave the first clue when she insisted that the child had never been away from her long enough to have had these experiences, but came directly home from school every afternoon for her tea, of which she habitually drank ten or twelve cups. The skilful questionings at the clinic, while clearly establishing the fact of a disordered mind, disclosed an astonishing knowledge of the habits of the underworld.

Even children who live in respectable neighborhoods and are guarded by careful parents so that their imaginations are not perverted, but only starved, constantly conduct a search for the magical and impossible which leads them into moral dangers. An astonishing number of them consult palmists, soothsayers, and fortune tellers. These dealers in futurity, who sell only love and riches, the latter often dependent upon the first, are sometimes in collusion with disreputable houses, and at the best make the path of normal living more difficult for their eager young patrons. There is something very pathetic in the sheepish, yet radiant, faces of the boy and girl, often together, who come out on the street from a dingy doorway which bears the palmist's sign of the spread-out hand. This remnant of primitive magic is all they can find with which to feed their eager imaginations, although the city offers libraries and galleries, crowned with man's later imaginative achievements. One hard-working girl of my acquaintance, told by a palmist that "diamonds were coming to her soon," afterwards accepted without a moment's hesitation a so-called diamond ring from a man whose improper attentions she had hitherto withstood.

In addition to these heedless young people, pulled into a sordid and vicious life through their very search for romance, are many little children ensnared by means of the most innocent playthings and pleasures of childhood. Perhaps one of the saddest aspects of the social evil as it exists to-day in the modern city, is the procuring of little girls who are too young to have received adequate instruction of any sort and whose natural safeguard of modesty and reserve has been broken down by the overcrowding of tenement house life. Any educator who has made a careful study of the children from the crowded districts is impressed with the numbers of them whose moral natures are apparently unawak-ened. While there are comparatively few of these non-moral children in any one neighborhood, in the entire city their number is far from negligible. Such children are used by disreputable people to invite their more normal playmates to house parties, which they attend again and again, lured by candy and fruit, until they gradually learn to trust the vicious hostess. The head of one such house, recently sent to the pen-itentiary upon charges brought against her by the Juvenile Protective Association, founded her large and successful business upon the activ-ities of three or four little girls who, although they had gradually come to understand her purpose, were apparently so chained to her by the goodies and favors which they received, that they were quite indiffer-ent to the fate of their little friends. Such children, when brought to the psychopathic clinic attached to the Chicago juvenile court, are some-times found to have incipient epilepsy or other physical disabilities from which their conduct may be at least partially accounted for. Some-times they come from respectable families, but more often from fam-ilies where they have been mistreated and where dissolute parents have given them neither affection nor protection. Many of these children whose relatives have obviously contributed to their delinquency are helped by the enforcement of the adult delinquency law.

One looks upon these hardened little people with a sense of apolo-gy that educational forces have not been able to break into their first ignorance of life before it becomes toughened into insensibility, and one knows that, whatever may be done for them later, because of this early neglect, they will probably always remain impervious to the gen-tler aspects of life, as if vice seared their tender minds with red-hot irons. Our public-school education is so nearly universal, that if the entire body of the teachers seriously undertook to instruct all Ameri-can youth in regard to this most important aspect of life, why should they not in time train their pupils to continence and self-direction, as they already discipline their minds with knowledge in regard to many other matters? Certainly the extreme youth of the victims of the white slave traffic, both boys and girls, places a great responsibility upon the educational forces of the community.

The state which supports the public school is also coming to the rescue of children through protective legislation. This is another illustration that the beginnings of social advance have often resulted from the efforts to defend the weakest and least-sheltered members of the community. The widespread movement which would protect children from premature labor, also prohibits them from engaging in occupations in which they are subjected to moral dangers. Several American cities have of late become much concerned over the temptations to which messenger boys, delivery boys, and newsboys are constantly subjected when their business takes them into vicious districts. The Chicago vice commission makes a plea for these "children of the night" that they shall be protected by law from those temptations which they are too young and too untrained to withstand. New York and Wisconsin are the only states which have raised the legal age of messenger boys employed late at night to twenty-one years. Under the inadequate sixteen-year limit, which regulates night work for children in Illinois, boys constantly come to grief through their familiarity with the social evil. One of these, a delicate boy of seventeen, had been put into the messenger service by his parents when their family doctor had recommended out-of-door work. Because he was well-bred and good-looking, he became especially popular with the inmates of disreputable houses. They gave him tips of a dollar and more when he returned from the errands which he had executed for them, such as buying candy, cocaine or morphine. He was inevitably flattered by their attentions and pleased with his own popularity. Although his mother knew that his duties as a messenger boy occasionally took him to disreputable houses, she fervently hoped his early training might keep him straight, but in the end realized the foolhardiness of subjecting an immature youth to these temptations. The vice commission report gives various detailed instances of similar experiences on the part of other lads, one of them being a high-school boy who was merely earning extra money as a messenger boy during the rush of Christmas week.

The regulations in Boston, New York, Cincinnati, Milwaukee and St. Louis for the safe-guarding of these children may be but a forecast of the care which the city will at last learn to devise for youth under special temptations. Because the various efforts made in Chicago to obtain adequate legislation for the protection of street-trading children have not succeeded, incidents like the following have not only occurred once, but are constantly repeated: a pretty little girl, the only child of a widowed mother, sold newspapers after school hours from the time she was seven years old. Because her home was near a vicious neighborhood and because the people in the disreputable hotels seldom asked for change when they bought a paper and good-naturedly gave her many little presents, her mother permitted her to gain a clientele within the district on the ground that she was too young to understand what she might see. This continued familiarity, in spite of her mother's admonitions, not to talk to her customers, inevitably resulted in so vitiating the standard of the growing girl, that at the age of fourteen she became an inmate of one of the houses. A similar instance concerns three little girls who habitually sold gum in one of the segregated districts. Because they had repeatedly been turned away by kind-hearted policemen who felt that they ought not to be in such a neighborhood, each one of these children had obtained a special permit from the mayor of the city in order to protect herself from "police interference." While the mayor had no actual authority to issue such permits, naturally the piece of paper bearing his name, when displayed by a child, checked the activity of the police officer. The incident was but one more example of the old conflict between mistaken kindness to the individual child in need of money, and the enforcement of those regulations which may seem to work a temporary hardship upon one child, but save a hundred others from entering occupations which can only lead into blind alleys. Because such occupations inevitably result in increasing the number of unemployables, the educational system itself must be challenged.

A royal commission has recently recommended to the English Parliament that "the legally permissible hours for the employment of boys be shortened, that they be required to spend the hours so set free, in physical and technological training, that the manufacturing of the unemployable may cease." Certainly we are justified in demanding from our educational system, that the interest and capacity of each child leaving school to enter industry, shall have been studied with reference to the type of work he is about to undertake. When vocational bureaus are properly connected with all the public schools, a girl will have an intelligent point of departure into her working life, and a place to which she may turn in time of need, for help and advice through those long and dangerous periods of unemployment which are now so inimical to her character.

This same British commission divided all of the unemployed, the under-employed, and the unemployable as the results of three types of trades: first, the subsidized labor trades, wherein women and children are paid wages insufficient to maintain them at the required standard of health and industrial efficiency, so that their wages must be supplemented by relatives or charity; second, labor deteriorating trades, which have sapped the energy, the capacity, the character, of workers; third, bare subsistence trades, where the worker is forced to such a low level in his standard of life that he continually falls below self-support. We have many trades of these three types in America, all of them demanding the work of young and untrained girls. Yet, in spite of the obvious dangers surrounding every girl who enters one of them, little is done to guide the multitude of children who leave school prematurely each year into reasonable occupations.

Unquestionably the average American child has received a more expensive education than has yet been accorded to the child of any other nation. The girls working in department stores have been in the public schools on an average of eight years, while even the factory girls, who so often leave school from the lower grades, have yet averaged six and two-tenths years of education at the public expense, before they enter industrial life. Certainly the community that has accomplished so much could afford them help and oversight for six and a half years longer, which is the average length of time that a working girl is employed. The state might well undertake this, if only to secure its former investment and to save that investment from utter loss.

Our generation, said to have developed a new enthusiasm for the possibilities of child life, and to have put fresh meaning into the phrase "children's rights," may at last have the courage to insist upon a child's right to be well born and to start in life with its tiny body free from disease. Certainly allied to this new understanding of child life and a part of the same movement is the new science of eugenics with its recently appointed university professors. Its organized societies publish an ever-increasing mass of information as to that which constitutes the inheritance of well-born children. When this new science makes clear to the public that those diseases which are a direct outcome of the social evil are clearly responsible for race deterioration, effective indignation may at last be aroused, both against the preventable infant mortality for which these diseases are responsible, and against the ghastly fact that the survivors among these afflicted children infect their contemporaries and hand on the evil heritage to another generation. Public societies for the prevention of blindness are continually distributing information on the care of new-born children and may at length answer that old, confusing question "Did this man sin or his parents, that he was born blind?" Such knowledge is becoming more widespread every day and the rising interest in infant welfare must in time re-act upon the very existence of the social evil itself.

This new public concern for the welfare of little children in certain American cities has resulted in a municipal milk supply; in many German cities, in free hospitals and nurseries. New York, Chicago, Boston and other large towns, employ hundreds of nurses each summer to instruct tenement-house mothers upon the care of little children. Doubtless all of this enthusiasm for the nurture of children will at last arouse public opinion in regard to the transmission of that one type of disease which thousands of them annually inherit, and which is directly traceable to the vicious living of their parents or grandparents. This slaughter of the innocents, this infliction of suffering upon the new-born, is so gratuitous and so unfair, that it is only a question of time until an outraged sense of justice shall be aroused on behalf of these children. But even before help comes through chivalric sentiments, governmental and municipal agencies will decline to spend the tax-payers' money for the relief of suffering infants, when by the exertion of the same authority they could easily provide against the possibility of the birth of a child so afflicted. It is obvious that the average tax-payer would be moved to demand the extermination of that form of vice which has been declared illegal, although it still flourishes by official connivance, did he once clearly apprehend that it is responsible for the existence of these diseases which cost him so dear. It is only his ignorance which makes him remain inert until each victim of the white slave traffic shall be avenged unto the third and fourth generation of them that bought her. It is quite possible that the tax-payer will himself contend that, as the state does not legalize a marriage without a license officially recorded, that the status of children may be clearly defined, so the state would need to go but one step further in the same direction, to insist upon health certificates from the applicant for a marriage license, that the health of future children might in a certain measure, be guaranteed. Whether or not this step may be predicted, the mere discussion of this matter in itself, is an indication of the changing public opinion, as is the fact that such legislation has already been enacted in two states, which are only now putting into action the recommendation made centuries ago by such social philosophers as Plato and Sir Thomas More. A sense of justice outraged by the wanton destruction of new-born children, may in time unite with that ardent tide of rising enthusiasm for the nurture of the young, until the old barriers of silence and inaction, behind which the social evil has so long intrenched itself, shall at last give way.

Certainly it will soon be found that the sentiment of pity, so recently aroused throughout the country on behalf of the victims of the white slave traffic, will be totally unable to afford them protection unless it becomes incorporated in government. It is possible that we are on the eve of a series of legislative enactments similar to those which resulted from the attempts to, regulate child labor. Through the entire course of the last century, in that anticipation of coming changes which does so much to bring changes about, the friends of the children were steadily engaged in making a new state, from the first child labor law passed in the English parliament in 1803 to the final passage of the so-called children's charter in 1909. During the long century of transforming pity into political action there was created that social sympathy which has become one of the greatest forces in modern legislation, and to which we may confidently appeal in this new crusade against the social evil.

Another point of similarity to the child labor movement is obvious, for the friends of the children early found that they needed much statistical information and that the great problem of the would-be reformer is not so much overcoming actual opposition—the passing of time gradually does that for him—as obtaining and formulating accurate knowledge and fitting that knowledge into the trend of his time. From this point of view and upon the basis of what has already been accomplished for "the protection of minors," the many recent investigations which have revealed the extreme youth of the victims of the white slave traffic, should make legislation on their behalf all the more feasible. Certainly no reformer could ever more legitimately make an emotional appeal to the higher sensibility of the public.

In the rescue homes recently opened in Chicago by the White Slave

Traffic Committee of the League of Cook County Clubs, the tender ages of the little girls who were brought there horrified the good clubwomen more than any other aspect of the situation. A number of the little inmates in the home wanted to play with dolls and several of them brought dolls of their own, which they had kept with them through all their vicissitudes. There is something literally heart-breaking in the thought of these little children who are ensnared and debauched when they are still young enough to have every right to protection and care. Quite recently I visited a home for semi-delinquent girls against each one of whom stood a grave charge involving the loss of her chastity. Upon each of the little white beds or on one of the stiff chairs standing by its side was a doll belonging to a delinquent owner still young enough to love and cherish this supreme toy of childhood. I had come to the home prepared to "lecture to the inmates." I remained to dress dolls with a handful of little girls who eagerly asked questions about the dolls I had once possessed in a childhood which seemed to them so remote. Looking at the little victims who supply the white slave trade, one is reminded of the burning words of Dr. Howard Kelly uttered in response to the demand that the social evil be legalized and its victims licensed. He says: "Where shall we look to recruit the ever-failing ranks of these poor creatures as they die yearly by the tens of thousands? Which of the little girls of our land shall we designate for this traffic? Mark their sweet innocence to-day as they run about in our streets and parks prattling and playing, ever busy about nothing; which of them shall we snatch as they approach maturity, to supply this foul mart?"

It is incomprehensible that a nation whose chief boast is its free public education, that a people always ready to respond to any moral or financial appeal made in the name of children, should permit this infamy against childhood to continue! Only the protection of all children from the menacing temptations which their youth is unable to withstand, will prevent some of them from falling victims to the white slave traffic; only when moral education is made effective and universal will there be hope for the actual abolition of commercialized vice. These are illustrations perhaps of that curious solidarity of which society is so rapidly becoming conscious.

5

Philanthropic Rescue
and Prevention

∂. There is no doubt that philanthropy often reflects and dramatizes the modern sensitiveness of the community in relation to a social wrong, because those engaged in the rescue of the victims are able to apprehend, through their daily experiences, many aspects of a recognized evil concerning which the public are ignorant and therefore indifferent. However ancient a wrong may be, in each generation it must become newly embodied in living people and the social custom into which it has hardened through the years, must be continued in individual lives. Unless the contemporaries of such unhappy individuals are touched to tenderness or stirred to indignation by the actual embodiments of the old wrong in their own generation, effective action cannot be secured.

The social evil has, on the whole, received less philanthropic effort than any other well-recognized menace to the community, largely because there is something peculiarly distasteful and distressing in personal acquaintance with its victims; a distaste and distress that sometimes leads to actual nervous collapse. A distinguished Englishman has recently written "that sober-minded people who, from motives of pity, have looked the hideous evil full in the face, have often asserted that nothing in their experience has seemed to threaten them so nearly with a loss of reason."

Nevertheless, this comparative lack of philanthropic effort is the more remarkable because the average age of the recruits to prostitution is between sixteen and eighteen years, the age at which girls are still minors under the law in respect to all matters of property. We allow a minor to determine for herself whether or not she will live this most abominable life, although if she resolve to be a thief she will, if possible, be apprehended and imprisoned; if she become a vagrant she will be restrained; even if she become a professional beggar, she will be interfered with; but the decision to lead this evil life, disastrous alike to herself and the community, although well known to the police, is openly permitted. If a man has seized upon a moment of weakness in a girl and obtained her consent, although she may thereafter be in dire need of help she is put outside all protection of the law. The courts assume that such a girl has deliberately decided for herself and that because she is not "of previous chaste life and character," she is lost to all decency. Yet every human being knows deep down in his heart that his own moral energy ebbs and flows, that he could not be judged fairly by his hours of defeat, and that after revealing moments of weakness, although shocked and frightened, he is the same human being, struggling as he did before. Nevertheless in some states, a little girl as young as ten years of age may make this irrevocable decision for herself.

Modern philanthropy, continually discovering new aspects of prostitution through the aid of economics, sanitary science, statistical research, and many other agencies, finds that this increase of knowledge inevitably leads it from the attempt to rescue the victims of white slavery to a consideration of the abolition of the monstrous wrong itself. At the present moment philanthropy is gradually impelled to a consideration of prostitution in relation to the welfare and the orderly existence of society itself. If the moral fire seems at times to be dying out of certain good old words, such as charity, it is filling with new warmth such words as social justice, which belong distinctively to our own time. It is also true that those for whom these words contain most of hope and warmth are those who have been long mindful of the old tasks and obligations, as if the great basic emotion of human compassion had more than held its own. Certainly the youth of many of the victims of the white slave traffic, and the helplessness of the older girls who find themselves caught in the grip of an enormous force which they cannot comprehend, make a most pitiful appeal. Philanthropy moreover discovers many young girls, who if they had not been rescued by protective agencies would have become permanent outcasts, although they would have entered a disreputable life through no fault of their own.

The illustrations in this chapter are all taken from the Juvenile Protective Association of Chicago in connection with its efforts to save girls from overwhelming temptation. Doubtless many other associations could offer equally convincing testimony, for in recent years the number of people to whom the very existence of the white slave traffic has become unendurable and who are determinedly working against it, has enormously increased.

A surprising number of country girls have been either brought to Chicago under false pretenses, or have been decoyed into an evil life very soon after their arrival in the city. Mr. Clifford Roe estimates that more than half of the girls who have been recruited into a disreputable life in Chicago have come from the farms and smaller towns in Illinois and from neighboring states. This estimate is borne out by the records of Paris and other metropolitan cities in which it is universally estimated that a little less than one-third of the prostitutes found in them, at any given moment, are city born.

The experience of a pretty girl who came to the office of the Juvenile Protective Association, a year ago, is fairly typical of the argument many of these country girls offer in their own defense. This girl had been a hotel chambermaid in an Iowa town where many of the traveling patrons of the hotel had made love to her, one of them occasionally offering her protection if she would leave with him. At first she indignantly refused, but was at length convinced that the acceptance of such offers must be a very general practice and that, whatever might be the custom in the country, no one in a city made personal inquiries. She finally consented to accompany a young man to Seattle, both because she wanted to travel and because she was discouraged in her attempts to "be good." A few weeks later, when in Chicago, she had left the young man, acting from what she considered a point of honor, as his invitation had been limited to the journey which was now completed. Feeling too disgraced to go home and under the glamour of the life of idleness she had been leading, she had gone voluntarily into a disreputable house, in which the police had found her and sent her to the Association. She could not be persuaded to give up her plan, but consented to wait for a few days to "think it over." As she was leaving the office in company with a representative of the Association, they met the young man, who had been distractedly searching for her and had just discovered her whereabouts. She was married the very same day and of course the Association never saw her again.

From the point of view of the traffickers in white slaves, it is much cheaper and safer to procure country girls after they have reached the city. Such girls are in constant danger because they are much more easily secreted than girls procured from the city. A country girl entering a vicious life quickly feels the disgrace and soon becomes too broken-spirited and discouraged to make any effort to escape into the unknown city which she believes to be full of horrors similar to those she has already encountered. She desires above all things to deceive her family at home, often sending money to them regularly and writing letters describing a fictitious life of hard work. Perhaps the most flagrant case with which the Association ever dealt, was that of two young girls who had come to Chicago from a village in West Virginia, hoping to earn large wages in order to help their families. They arrived in the city penniless, having been robbed en route of their one slender purse. As they stood in the railway station, utterly bewildered, they were accosted by a young man who presented the advertising card of a boarding-house and offered to take them there. They quite innocently accepted his invitation, but an hour later, finding themselves in a locked room, they became frightened and realized they had been duped. Fortunately the two agile country girls had no difficulty in jumping from a second-story window, but upon the street they were of course much too frightened to speak to anyone again and wandered about for hours. The house from which they had escaped bore the sign "rooms to rent," and they therefore carefully avoided all houses whose placards offered shelter. Finally, when they were desperate with hunger, they went into a saloon for a "free lunch," not in the least realizing that they were expected to take a drink in order to receive it. A policeman, seeing two young girls in a saloon "without escort," arrested them and took them to the nearest station where they spent the night in a wretched cell.

At the hearing the next morning, where, much frightened, they gave a very incoherent account of their adventures, the judge fined them each fifteen dollars and costs, and as they were unable to pay the fine, they were ordered sent to the city prison. When they were escorted from the court room, another man approached them and offered to pay their fines if they would go with him. Frightened by their former experience, they stoutly declined his help, but were over-persuaded by his graphic portrayal of prison horrors and the disgrace that their imprisonment would bring upon "the folks at home." He also made clear that when they came out of prison, thirty days later, they would be no better off than they were now, save that they would have the added stigma of being jail-birds. The girls at last reluctantly consented to go with him, when a representative of the Juvenile Protective Association, who had followed them from the court room and had listened to the conversation, insisted upon the prompt arrest of the white slave trader. When the entire story, finally secured from the girls, was related to the judge, he reversed his decision, fined the man $100.00, which he was abundantly able to pay, and insisted that the girls be sent back to their mothers in Virginia. They were farmers' daughters, strong and capable of taking care of themselves in an environment that they understood, but in constant danger because of their ignorance of city life.

The methods employed to secure city girls must be much more subtle and complicated than those employed with the less sophisticated country girl. Although the city girl, once procured, is later allowed more freedom than is accorded either to a country girl or to an immigrant girl, every effort is made to demoralize her completely before she enters the life. Because she may, at any moment, escape into the city which she knows so well, it is necessary to obtain her inner consent. Those whose profession it is to procure girls for the white slave trade apparently find it possible to decoy and demoralize most easily that city girl whose need for recreation has led her to the disreputable public dance hall or other questionable places of amusement.

Gradually those philanthropic agencies that are endeavoring to be of service to the girls learn to know the dangers in these places. Many parents are utterly indifferent or ignorant of the pleasures that their children find for themselves. From the time these children were five years old, such parents were accustomed to see them take care of themselves on the street and at school, and it seems but natural that when the children are old enough to earn money, they should be able to find their own amusements.

The girls are attracted to the unregulated dance halls not only by a love of pleasure but by a sense of adventure, and it is in these places that they are most easily recruited for a vicious life. Unfortunately there are three hundred and twenty-eight public dance halls in Chicago, one hundred and ninety of them connect directly with saloons, while liquor is openly sold in most of the others. This consumption of liquor enormously increases the danger to young people. A girl after a long day's work is easily induced to believe that a drink will dispel her lassitude. There is plenty of time between the dances to persuade her, as the intermissions are long, fifteen to twenty minutes, and the dances short, occupying but four or five minutes; moreover the halls are hot and dusty and it is almost impossible to obtain a drink of water. Often the entire purpose of the dance hall, with its carefully arranged intermissions, is the selling of liquor to the people it has brought together. After the girl has begun to drink, the way of the procurer, who is often in league with the "spieler" who frequents the dance hall, is comparatively easy. He assumes one of two roles, that of the sympathetic older man or that of the eager young lover. In the character of the former, he tells "the down-trodden working girl" that her wages are a mere pittance and that he can procure a better place for her with higher wages if she will trust him. He often makes allusions to the shabbiness or cheapness of her clothing and considers it "a shame that such a pretty girl cannot dress better." In the second role he apparently falls in love with her, tells of his rich parents, complaining that they want him to marry, "a society swell," but that he really prefers a working girl like herself. In either case he establishes friendly relations, exalted in the girl's mind, through the excitement of the liquor and the dance, into a new sense of intimate understanding and protection.

Later in the evening, she leaves the hall with him for a restaurant because, as he truthfully says, she is exhausted and in need of food. At the supper, however, she drinks much more, and it is not surprising that she is at last persuaded that it is too late to go home and in the end consents to spend the rest of the night in a nearby lodging house. Six young girls, each accompanied by a "spieler" from a dance hall, were recently followed to a chop suey restaurant and then to a lodging-house, which the police were instigated to raid and where the six girls, more or less intoxicated, were found. If no one rescues the girl after such an experience, she sometimes does not return home at all, or if she does, feels herself initiated into a new world where it is possible to obtain money at will, to easily secure the pleasures it brings, and she comes at length to consider herself superior to her less sophisticated companions. Of course this latter state of mind is untenable for any length of time and the girl is soon found openly leading a disreputable life.

The girls attending the cheap theatres and the vaudeville shows are most commonly approached through their vanity. They readily listen to the triumphs of a stage career, sure to be attained by such a "good looker," and a large number of them follow a young man to the woman with whom he is in partnership, under the promise of being introduced to a theatrical manager. There are also theatrical agencies in league with disreputable places, who advertise for pretty girls, promising large salaries. Such an agency operating with a well-known "near theatre" in the state capital was recently prosecuted in Chicago and its license revoked. In this connection the experience of two young English girls is not unusual. They were sisters possessed of an extraordinary skill in juggling, who were brought to this country by a relative acting as their manager. Although he exploited them for his own benefit for three years, paying them the most meager salaries and supplying them with the simplest living in the towns which they "toured," he had protected them from all immorality, and they had preserved the clean living of the family of acrobats to which they belonged. Last October, when appearing in San Francisco, the girls, then sixteen and seventeen years of age; demanded more pay than the dollar and twenty cents a week each had been receiving, representing the five shillings with which they had started from home. The manager, who had become discouraged with his American experience, refused to accede to their demands, gave them each a ticket for Chicago, and heartlessly turned them adrift. Arriving in the city, they quite naturally at once applied to a theatrical agency, through which they were sent to a disreputable house where a vaudeville program was given each night. Delighted that they had found work so quickly, they took the position in good faith. During the very first performance, however, they became frightened by the conduct of the girls who preceded them on the program and by the hilarity of the audience. They managed to escape from the dressing-room, where they were waiting their turn, and on the street appealed to the first policeman, who brought them to the

Juvenile Protective Association. They were detained for several days as witnesses against the theatrical agency, entering into the legal prosecution with that characteristic British spirit which is ever ready to protest against an imposition, before they left the city with a travelling company, each on a weekly salary of twenty dollars.

The methods pursued on excursion boats are similar to those of the dance halls, in that decent girls are induced to drink quantities of liquor to which they are unaccustomed. On the high seas, liquor is sold usually in original packages, which enormously increases the amount consumed. It is not unusual to see a boy and girl drinking between them an entire bottle of whiskey. Some of these excursion boats carry five thousand people and in the easy breakdown of propriety which holiday-making often implies, and the absence of police, to which city young people are unaccustomed, the utmost freedom and license is often indulged in. Thus the lake excursions, one of the most delightful possibilities for recreation in Chicago, through lack of proper policing and through the sale of liquor, are made a menace to thousands of young people to whom they should be a great resource.

When a philanthropic association, with a knowledge of the commercial exploitation of youth's natural response to gay surroundings, attempts to substitute innocent recreation, it finds the undertaking most difficult. In Chicago the Juvenile Protective Association, after a thorough investigation of public dance halls, amusement parks, five-cent theatres, and excursion boats, is insisting upon more vigorous enforcement of the existing legislation, and is also urging further legal regulation; Kansas City has instituted a Department of Public Welfare with power to regulate places of amusement; a New York committee has established model dance halls; Milwaukee is urging the appointment of commissions on public recreation, while New York and Columbus have already created them.

Perhaps nothing in actual operation is more valuable than the small parks of Chicago in which the large halls are used every evening for dancing and where outdoor sports, swimming pools and gymnasiums daily attract thousands of young people. Unless cities make some such provision for their youth, those who sell the facilities for amusement in order to make a profit will continue to exploit the normal desire of all young people for recreation and pleasure. The city of Chicago contains at present eight hundred and fourteen thousand minors, all eager for pleasure. It is not surprising that commercial enterprise undertakes to supply this demand and that penny arcades, slot machines, candy stores, ice-cream parlors, moving-picture shows, skating rinks, cheap theatres and dance halls are trying to attract young people with every device known to modern advertising. Their promoters are, of course, careless of the moral effect upon their young customers if they can but secure their money. Until municipal provisions adequately meet this need, philanthropic and social organizations must be committed to the establishment of more adequate recreational facilities.

Although many dangers are encountered by the pleasure-loving girl who demands that each evening shall bring her some measure of recreation, a large number of girls meet with difficulties and temptations while soberly at work. Many of these tempted girls are newly-arrived immigrant girls between the ages of sixteen and twenty, who find their first work in hotels. Polish girls especially are utilized in hotel kitchens and laundries, and for the interminable scrubbing of halls and lobbies where a knowledge of the English language is not necessary, but where their peasant strength is in demand. The work is very heavy and fatiguing and until the Illinois law limited the work of women to ten hours a day, it often lasted late into the night. Even now the girls report themselves so tired that at the end of the day, they crowd into the dormitories and fall upon their beds undressed. When food and shelter is given them, their wages are from $14.00 to $18.00 a month, most of which is usually sent back to the old country, that the remaining members of the family may be brought to America. Such positions are surrounded by temptations of every sort. Even the hotel housekeepers, who are honestly trying to protect the girls, admit that it is impossible to do it adequately. One of these housekeepers recently said "that it takes a girl who knows the world to work in any hotel," and regretted that the sophisticated English-speaking girl who might protect herself, was unable to endure the hard work. She added that as soon as a girl learned English she promoted her from the laundry to the halls and from there to the position of chambermaid, but that the latter position was the most dangerous of all, as the girls were constantly exposed to insults from the guests. In the less respectable hotels these newly-arrived immigrant girls, inevitably seeing a great deal of the life of the underworld and the apparent ease with which money may be earned in illicit ways, find their first impression of the moral standards of life in America most bewildering. One young Polish girl had worked for two years in a down-town hotel, and had steadfastly resisted all improper advances even sometimes by the aid of her own powerful fist. She yielded at last to the suggestions of the life about her when she received a telegram from Ellis Island stating that her mother had arrived in New York, but was too ill to be sent on to Chicago. All of her money had gone for the steamer ticket and as the thought of her old country mother, ill and alone among strangers, was too much for her long fortitude, she made the best bargain possible with the head waiter whose importunities she had hitherto resisted, accepted the little purse the other Polish girls in the hotel collected for her and arrived in New York only to find that her mother had died the night before.

The simple obedience to parents on the part of these immigrant girls, working in hotels and restaurants, often miscarries pathetically. Their unspoiled human nature, not yet immune to the poisons of city life, when thrust into the midst of that unrelieved drudgery which lies at the foundation of all complex luxury, often results in the most fatal reactions. A young German woman, the proprietor of what is considered a successful "house" in the most notorious district in Chicago, traces her career directly to a desperate attempt to conform to the standard of "bringing home good wages" maintained by her numerous brothers and sisters. One requirement of her home was rigid: all money earned by a child must be paid into the family income until "legal age" was attained. The slightly neurotic, very pretty girl of seventeen heartily detested the dish-washing in a restaurant, which constituted her first place in America, and quite honestly declared that the heavy lifting was beyond her strength. Such insubordination was not tolerated at home, and every Saturday night when her meager wages, reduced by sick days "off," were compared with what the others brought in, she was regularly scolded, "sometimes slapped," by her parents, jeered at by her more vigorous sisters and bullied by her brothers. She tried to shorten her hours by doing "rush-work" as a waitress at noon, but she found this still beyond her strength, and worst of all, the pay of two dollars and a half insufficient to satisfy her mother. Confiding her troubles to the other waitresses, one of them good-naturedly told her how she could make money through appointments in a nearby disreputable hotel, and so take home an increased amount of money easily called "a raise in wages." So strong was the habit of obedience, that the girl continued to take money home every Saturday night until her eighteenth birthday, in spite of the fact that she gave up the restaurant in less than six weeks after her first experience. Although all of this happened ten years ago and the German mother is long since dead, the daughter bitterly ended the story with the infamous hope that "the old lady was now suffering the torments of the lost, for making me what I am." Such a girl was subjected to temptations to which society has no right to expose her.

A dangerous cynicism regarding the value of virtue, a cynicism never so unlovely as in the young, sometimes seizes a girl who, because of long hours and overwork, has been unable to preserve either her health or spirits and has lost all measure of joy in life. That this premature cynicism may be traced to an unhappy and narrow childhood is suggested by the fact that a large number of these girls come from families in which there has been little affection and the poor substitute of parental tyranny.

A young Italian girl who earned four dollars a week in a tailor shop pulling out bastings, when asked why she wore a heavy woolen gown on one of the hottest days of last summer, replied that she was obliged to earn money for her clothes by scrubbing for the neighbors after hours; that she had found no such work lately and that her father would not allow her anything from her wages for clothes or for carfare, because he was buying a house.

This parental control sometimes exercised in order to secure all of a daughter's wages, is often established with the best intentions in the world. I recall a French dressmaker who had frugally supported her two daughters until they were of working age, when she quite naturally expected them to conform to the careful habits of living necessary during her narrow years. In order to save carfare, she required her daughters to walk a long distance to the department store in which one was a bundle wrapper and the other a clerk at the ribbon counter. They dressed in black as being the most economical color and a penny spent in pleasure was never permitted. One day a young man who was buying ribbon from the older girl gave her a yard with the remark that she was much too young and pretty to be so somberly dressed. She wore the ribbon at work, never of course at home, but it opened a vista of delightful possibilities and she eagerly accepted a pair of gloves the following week from the same young man, who afterwards asked her to dine with him. This was the beginning of a winter of surreptitious pleasures on the part of the two sisters. They were shrewd enough never to be out later than ten o'clock and always brought home so-called overtime pay to their mother. In the spring the older girl, finding herself worn out by her dissipation and having resolved to cut loose from her home, came to the office of the Juvenile Protective Association to ask help for her younger sister. It was discovered that the mother was totally ignorant of the semi-professional life her daughters had been leading. She reiterated over and over again that she had always guarded them carefully and had given them no money to spend. It took months of constant visiting on the part of a representative of the Association before she was finally persuaded to treat the younger girl more generously.

While this family is fairly typical of those in which over-restraint is due to the lack of understanding, it is true that in most cases the family tyranny is exercised by an old-country father in an honest attempt to guard his daughter against the dangers of a new world. The worst instances, however, are those in which the father has fallen into the evil ways of drink, and not only demands all of his daughter's wages, but treats her with great brutality when those wages fall below his expectations. Many such daughters have come to grief because they have been afraid to go home at night when their wage envelopes contained less than usual, either because a new system of piece work had reduced the amount or because, in a moment of weakness, they had taken out five cents with which to attend a show, or ten cents for the much-desired pleasure of riding back and forth the full length of an elevated railroad, or because they had in a thirsty moment taken out a nickel for a drink of soda water, or worst of all, had fallen a victim to the installment plan of buying a new hat or a pair of shoes. These girls, in their fear of beatings and scoldings, although they are sure of shelter and food and often have a mother who is trying to protect them from domestic storms, have almost no money for clothing, and are inevitably subject to moments of sheer revolt, their rebellion intensified by the fact that after a girl earns her own money and is accustomed to come and go upon the streets as an independent wage earner, she finds unsympathetic control much harder to bear than do schoolgirls of the same age who have never broken the habits of their childhood and are still economically dependent upon their parents.

In spite of the fact that domestic service is always suggested by the average woman as an alternative for the working girl whose life is beset with danger, the federal report on "Women and Child Wage Earners in the United States" gives the occupation of the majority of girls who go wrong as that of domestic service, and in this it confirms the experience of every matron in a rescue home and the statistics in the maternity wards of the public hospitals. The report suggests that the danger comes from the general conditions of work: "These general conditions are the loneliness of the life, the lack of opportunities for making friends and securing recreation and amusement in safe surroundings, the monotonous and uninteresting nature of the work done as these untrained girls do it, the lack of external stimulus to pride and self-respect, and the absolutely unguarded state of the girl, except when directly under the eye of her mistress."

In addition to these reasons, the girls realize that the opportunities for marriage are less in domestic service than in other occupations, and after all, the great business of youth is securing a mate, as the young instinctively understand. Unlike the working girl who lives at home and constantly meets young men of her own neighborhood and factory life, the girl in domestic service is brought into contact with very few possible lovers. Even the men of her former acquaintance, however slightly Americanized, do not like to call on a girl in someone else's kitchen, and find the entire situation embarrassing. The girl's mistress knows that for her own daughters mutual interests and recreation are the natural foundations for friendship with young men, which may or may not lead to marriage, but which is the prerogative of every young girl. The mistress does not, however, apply this worldly wisdom to the maid in her service, only eighteen or nineteen years old, utterly dependent upon her for social life save during one afternoon and evening a week.

The majority of domestics are employed in families where there is only one, and the tired and dispirited girl, often without a taste for reading, spends many lonely hours. That most fundamental and powerful of all instincts has therefore no chance for diffusion or social expression and like all confined forces, tends to degenerate. The girl is equipped with no weapon with which to contend with those poisonous images which arise from the senses, and these images, bred of fatigue and loneliness, make a girl an easy victim. This is especially true of the colored girl, who because of her traditions, is often treated with so little respect by white men, that she is constantly subjected to insult. Even the colored servants in the New York apartment houses, who live at home and thus avoid this loneliness, because their hours extend until nine in the evening, are obliged to seek their pleasures late into the night. American cities offer occupation to more colored women than colored men and this surplus of women, in some cities as large as one hundred and thirty or forty women to one hundred men, affords an opportunity to the procurer which he quickly seizes. He is often in league with certain employment bureaus, who make a business of advancing the railroad or boat fare to colored girls coming from the South to enter into domestic service. The girl, in debt and unused to the city, is often put into a questionable house and kept there until her debt is paid many times over. In some respects her position is not unlike that of the imported white slave, for although she has the inestimable advantage of speaking the language, she finds it even more difficult to have her story credited. This contemptuous attitude places her at a disadvantage, for so universally are colored girls in domestic service suspected of blackmail that the average court is slow to credit their testimony when it is given against white men. The field of employment for colored girls is extremely limited. They are seldom found in factories and workshops. They are not wanted in department stores nor even as waitresses in hotels. The majority of them therefore are engaged in domestic service and often find the position of maid in a house of prostitution or of chambermaid in a disreputable hotel, the best-paying position open to them.

When a girl who has been in domestic service loses her health, or for any other reason is unable to carry on her occupation, she is often curiously detached and isolated, because she has had so little opportunity for normal social relationships and friendships. One of the saddest cases ever brought to my personal knowledge was that of an orphan Norwegian girl who, coming to America at the age of seventeen, had been for three years in one position as general housemaid, during which time she had drawn only such part of her wages as was necessary for her simple clothing. At the end of three years, when she was sent to a public hospital with nervous prostration, her employer refused to pay her accumulated wages, on the ground that owing to her ill health she had been of little use during the last year. When she left the hospital, practically penniless, advised by the physician to find some outdoor work, she sold a patented egg-beater for six months, scarcely earning enough for her barest necessities and in constant dread lest she could not "keep respectable." When she was found wandering upon the street she not only had no capital with which to renew her stock, but had been without food for two days and had resolved to drown herself. Every effort was made to restore the half-crazed girl, but unfortunately hospital restraint was not considered necessary, and a month later, in spite of the vigilance of her new employer, her body was taken from the lake. One more of those gentle spirits who had found the problem of life insoluble, had sought refuge in death.

A surprising number of suicides occur among girls who have been in domestic service, when they discover that they have been betrayed by their lovers. Perhaps nothing is more astonishing than the attitude of the mistress when the situation of such a forlorn girl is discovered, and it would be interesting to know how far this attitude has influenced these girls either to suicide or to their reckless choice of a disreputable life, which statistics show so many of their number have elected. The mistress almost invariably promptly dismisses such a girl, assuring her that she is disgraced forever and too polluted to remain for another hour in a good home. In full command of the situation, she usually succeeds in convincing the wretched girl that she is irreparably ruined. Her very phraseology, although unknown to herself, is a remnant of that earlier historic period when every woman was obliged in her own person to protect her home and to secure the status of her children. The indignant woman is trying to exercise alone that social restraint which should have been exercised by the community and which would have naturally protected the girl, if she had not been so withdrawn from it, in order to serve exclusively the interests of her mistress's family. Such a woman seldom follows the ruined girl through the dreary weeks after her dismissal; her difficulty in finding any sort of work, the ostracism of her former friends added to her own self-accusation, the poverty and loneliness, the final ten days in the hospital, and the great temptation which

comes after that, to give away her child. The baby farmer who haunts
the public hospitals for such cases tells her that upon the payment of
forty or fifty dollars, he will take care of the child for a year and that
"maybe it won't live any longer than that," and unless the hospital is
equipped with a social service department, such as the one at the Massachusetts General, the girl leaves it weak and low-spirited and too broken to care what becomes of her. It is in moments such as these that
many a poor girl, convinced that all the world is against her, decides to
enter a disreputable house. Here at least she will find food and shelter,
she will not be despised by the other inmates and she can earn money
for the support of her child. Often she has received the address of such
a house from one of her companions in the maternity ward where,
among the fifty per cent of the unmarried mothers, at least two or three
sophisticated girls are always to be found, eager to "put wise" the girls
who are merely unfortunate. Occasionally a girl who follows such bane-
ful advice still insists upon keeping her child. I recall a pathetic case in
the juvenile court of Chicago when such a mother of a five-year-old
child was pronounced by the judge to be an "improper guardian." The
agonized woman was told that she might retain her child if she would
completely change her way of life; but she insisted that such a requirement was impossible, that she had no other means of earning her living, and that she had become too idle and broken for regular work. The
child clung piteously to the mother, and, having gathered from the evidence that she was considered "bad," assured the judge over and over
again that she was "the bestest mother in the world." The poor mother, who had begun her wretched mode of life for her child's sake, found
herself so demoralized by her hideous experiences that she could not
leave the life, even for the sake of the same child, still her most precious
possession. Only six years before, this mother had been an honest girl
cheerfully working in the household of a good woman, whose sense of
duty had expressed itself in dismissing "the outcast."

These discouraged girls, who so often come from domestic service
to supply the vice demands of the city, are really the last representatives
of those thousands of betrayed girls who for many years met the entire
demand of the trade; for, while a procurer of some sort has performed
his office for centuries, only in the last fifty years has the white slave
market required the services of extended business enterprises in order

to keep up the supply. Previously the demand had been largely met by the girls who had voluntarily entered a disreputable life because they had been betrayed. While the white slave traffic was organized primarily for profit it could of course never have flourished unless there had been a dearth of these discouraged girls. Is it not also significant that the surviving representatives of the girls who formerly supplied the demand are drawn most largely from the one occupation which is farthest from the modern ideal of social freedom and self-direction? Domestic service represents, in the modern world, more nearly than any other of the gainful occupations open to women, the ancient labor conditions under which woman's standard of chastity was developed and for so long maintained. It would seem obvious that both the girl over-restrained at home, as well as the girl in domestic service, had been too much withdrawn from the healthy influence of public opinion, and it is at least significant that domestic control has so broken down that the girls most completely under its rule are shown to be those in the greatest danger. Such a statement undoubtedly needs the modification that the girls in domestic service are frequently those who are unadapted to skilled labor and are least capable of taking care of themselves, yet the fact remains that they are belated morally as well as industrially. As they have missed the industrial discipline that comes from regular hours of systematized work, so they have missed the moral training of group solidarity, the ideals and restraints which the friendships and companionships of other working girls would have brought them.

When the judgment of her peers becomes not less firm but more kindly, the self-supporting girl will have a safeguard and restraint many times more effective than the individual control which has become so inadequate, or the family discipline that, with the best intentions in the world, cannot cope with existing social conditions. The most perplexing case that comes before the philanthropic organizations trying to aid and rescue the victims of the white slave traffic, is of the type which involves a girl who has been secured by the trafficker when so lonely, detached and discouraged that she greedily seized whatever friendship was offered her. Such a girl has been so eager for affection that she clings to even the wretched simulacrum of it, afforded by the man who calls himself her "protector," and she can only be permanently detached from the life to which he holds her, when she is put under the influence of more genuine affections and interests. That is doubtless one reason it is always more possible to help the girl who has become the mother of a child. Although she unjustly faces a public opinion much more severe than that encountered by the childless woman who also endeavors to "reform," the mother's sheer affection and maternal absorption enables her to overcome the greater difficulties more easily than the other woman, without the new warmth of motive, overcomes the lesser ones. The Salvation Army in their rescue homes have long recognized this need for an absorbing interest, which should involve the Magdalen's deepest affections and emotions, and therefore often utilize the rescued girl to save others.

Certainly no philanthropic association, however rationalistic and suspicious of emotional appeal, can hope to help a girl once overwhelmed by desperate temptation, unless it is able to pull her back into the stream of kindly human fellowship and into a life involving normal human relations. Such an association must needs remember those wise words of Count Tolstoy: "We constantly think that there are circumstances in which a human being can be treated without affection, and there are no such circumstances."

6

Increased Social Control

꤯ When certain groups in a community, to whom a social wrong has
become intolerable, prepare for definite action against it, they almost
invariably discover unexpected help from contemporaneous social
movements with which they later find themselves allied. The most immediate help in this new campaign against the social evil will probably come thus indirectly from those streams of humanitarian effort
which are ever widening and which will in time slowly engulf into their
rising tide of enthusiasm for human betterment, even the victims of
the white slave traffic.

Foremost among them is the world-wide movement to preserve and
prolong the term of human life, coupled with the determination on the
part of the medical profession to eliminate all forms of germ diseases.
The same physicians and sanitarians who have practically rid the modern city of small-pox and cholera and are eliminating tuberculosis, well
know that the social evil is directly responsible for germ diseases more
prevalent than any of the others, and also communicable. Over and over
again in the history of large cities, Vienna, Paris, St. Louis, the medical
profession has been urged to control the diseases resulting from the
commercialized vice which the municipal authorities themselves permitted. But the experiments in segregation, in licensed systems, and
certification have not been considered successful. The medical profession, hitherto divided in opinion as to the feasibility of such undertak-
ings, is virtually united in the conclusion that so long as commercialized vice exists, physicians cannot guarantee a city against the spread
of the contagious poison generated by it, which is fatal alike to the in-

dividual and to his offspring. The medical profession agrees that, as the victims of the social evil inevitably become the purveyors of germ diseases of a very persistent and incurable type, safety in this regard lies only in the extinction of commercialized vice. They point out the indirect ways in which this contagion can spread exactly as any other can, but insist that its control is enormously complicated by the fact that the victims of these diseases are most unwilling to be designated and quarantined. The medical profession is at last taking the position that the community wishing to protect itself against this contagion will in the end be driven to the extermination of the very source itself. A well-known authority states the one breeding-place of these disease germs, without exception, is the social institution designated as prostitution, but, once bred and cultivated there, they then spread through the community, attacking alike both the innocent and the guilty.

We can imagine, after a dozen years of vigorous and able propaganda of this opinion on the part of public-spirited physicians and sanitarians, that a city might well appeal to the medical profession to exterminate prostitution on the very ground that it is a source of constant danger to the health and future of the community. Such a city might readily give to the board of health ordered to undertake this extermination more absolute authority than is now accorded to it in a smallpox epidemic. Of course, no city could reach such a view unless the education of the public proceeded much more rapidly than at present, although the newly-established custom of careful medical examination of school-children and of employees in factories and commercial establishments must result in the discovery of many such cases, and in the end adequate provision must be made for their isolation. A child was recently discovered in a Chicago school with an open sore upon her lip, which made her a most dangerous source of infection. She was just fourteen years of age, too old to be admitted into that most pathetic and most unlovely of all children's wards, where children must suffer for "the sins of their fathers," and too young and innocent to be put into the women's ward in which the public takes care of those wrecks of dissolute living who are no longer valuable to the commerce which once secured them, and have become merely worthless stock which pays no dividend. The disease of the little girl was in too virulent a stage to admit her to that convalescent home lately established in Chicago for those infected children who are dismissed from the county hospital, but whom it is impossible to return to their old surroundings. A philanthropic association was finally obliged, to pay her board for weeks to a woman who carefully followed instructions as to her treatment. This is but one example of a child who was discovered and provided for, but it is evident that the public cannot long remain indifferent to the care of such cases when it has already established the means for detecting them. In twenty-seven months over six hundred children passed through this most piteous children's ward in Chicago's public hospital. All but twenty-nine of these children were under ten years of age, and doubtless a number of them had been victims of that wretched tradition that a man afflicted with this incurable disease might cure himself at the expense of innocence.

Crusades against other infectious diseases, such as small-pox and cholera, imply well-considered sanitary precautions, dependent upon widespread education and an aroused public opinion. To establish such education and to arouse the public in regard to this present menace apparently presents insuperable difficulties. Many newspapers, so ready to deal with all other forms of vice and misery, never allow these evils to be mentioned in their columns except in the advertisements of quack remedies; the clergy, unlike the founder of the Christian religion and the early apostles, seldom preach against the sin of which these contagions are an inevitable consequence: the physicians, bound by a rigorous medical etiquette, tell nothing of the prevalence of these maladies, use a confusing nomenclature in the hospitals, and write only contributory causes upon the very death certificates of the victims.

Yet it is easy to predict that a society committed to the abolition of infectious germs, to a higher degree of public health, and to a better standard of sanitation will not forever permit these highly communicable diseases to spread unchecked in its midst, and that a public, convinced that sanitary science, properly supported, might rid our cities of this type of disease, will at length insist upon its accomplishment. When we consider the many things undertaken in the name of health and sanitation it becomes easy to make the prediction, for public health is a magic word which ever grows more potent, as society realizes that the very existence of the modern city would be an impossibility had it not been discovered that the health of the individual is largely controlled by the hygienic condition of his surroundings. Since the first commission to inquire into the conditions of great cities was appointed in Manchester in 1844, sanitary science, both in knowledge and municipal authority, has progressed until advocates of the most advanced measures in city hygiene and preventive sanitary science boldly state that neglected childhood and neglected disease are the most potent causes of social insufficiency.

Certainly a plea could be made for the women and children who are often the innocent victims of these diseases. Quite recently in Chicago there was brought to my attention the incredibly pathetic plight of a widow with four children who was in such constant fear of spreading the infection for which her husband had been responsible, that she touchingly offered to leave her children forevermore, if there was no other way to save them from the horrible suffering she herself was enduring. In spite of thousands of such cases Utah is the pioneer and only state with a law which requires that this infection shall be reported and controlled, as are other contagious maladies, and which also authorizes boards of health to take adequate measures in order to secure protection.

Another humanitarian movement from which assistance will doubtless come to the crusade against the social evil, is the great movement against alcoholism with its recent revival in every civilized country of the world. A careful scientist has called alcohol the indispensable vehicle of the business transacted by the white slave traders, and has asserted that without its use this trade could not long continue. Whoever has tried to help a girl making an effort to leave the irregular life she has been leading, must have been discouraged by the victim's attempts to overcome the habit of using alcohol and drugs. Such a girl has commonly been drawn into the life in the first place when under the influence of liquor and has continued to drink that she might be able to live through each day. Furthermore, the drinking habit grows upon her because she is constantly required to sell liquor and to be "treated."

It is estimated that the liquor sold by such girls nets a profit to the trade of two hundred and fifty per cent over and above the girl's own commission. Chicago made at least one honest effort to divorce the sale of liquor from prostitution, when the superintendent of police last year ruled that no liquor should be sold in any disreputable house. The difficulty of enforcing such an order is greatly increased because such houses, as well as the questionable dance halls, commonly obtain a special permit to sell liquor under a federal license, which is not only cheaper than the saloon license obtained from the city, but has the added advantage to the holder that he can sell after one o'clock in the morning, at which time the city closes all saloons.

The aggregate annual profit of the two hundred and thirty-six disorderly saloons recently investigated in Chicago by the Vice Commission was $4,307,000. This profit on the sale of liquor can be traced all along the line in connection with the white slave traffic and is no less disastrous from the point of view of young men than of the girls. Even a slight exhilaration from alcohol relaxes the moral sense and throws a sentimental or adventurous glamor over an aspect of life from which a decent young man would ordinarily recoil, and its continued use stimulates the senses at the very moment when the intellectual and moral inhibitions are lessened. May we not conclude that both chastity and self-restraint are more firmly established in the modern city than we realize, when the white slave traders find it necessary both forcibly to detain their victims and to ply young men with alcohol that they may profit thereby? General Bingham, who as Police Commissioner of New York certainly knew whereof he spoke, says "There is not enough depravity in human nature to keep alive this very large business. The immorality of women arid the brutishness of men have to be persuaded, coaxed and constantly stimulated in order to keep the social evil in its present state of business prosperity."

We may soberly hope that some of the experiments made by governmental and municipal authorities to control and regulate the sale of liquor will at last meet with such a measure of success that the existence of public prostitution, deprived of its artificial stimulus of alcohol, will in the end be imperilled. The Chicago Vice Commission has made a series of valuable suggestions for the regulation of saloons and for the separation of the sale of liquor from dance halls and from all other places known as recruiting grounds for the white slave traffic. There is still need for a much wider and more thorough education of the public in regard to the historic connection between commercialized vice and alcoholism, of the close relation between politics and the liquor interests, behind which the social evil so often entrenches itself.

In addition to the movements against germ diseases and the suppression of alcoholism, both of which are mitigating the hard fate of the victims of the white slave traffic, other public movements mysteriously affecting all parts of the social order will in time threaten the very existence of commercialized vice. First among these, perhaps, is the equal suffrage movement. On the horizon everywhere are signs that woman will soon receive the right to exercise political power, and it is believed that she will show her efficiency most conspicuously in finding means for enhancing and preserving human life, if only as the result of her age-long experiences. That primitive maternal instinct, which has always been as ready to defend as it has been to nurture, will doubtless promptly grapple with certain crimes connected with the white slave traffic; women with political power would not brook that men should live upon the wages of captured victims, should openly hire youths to ruin and debase young girls, should be permitted to transmit poison to unborn children. Life is full of hidden remedial powers which society has not yet utilized, but perhaps nowhere is the waste more flagrant than in the matured deductions and judgments of the women, who are constantly forced to share the social injustices which they have no recognized power to alter. If political rights were once given to women, if the situation were theirs to deal with as a matter of civic responsibility, one cannot imagine that the existence of the social evil would remain unchallenged in its semi-legal protection. Those women who are already possessed of political power have in many ways registered their conscience in regard to it. The Norwegian women, for instance, have guaranteed to every illegitimate child the right of inheritance to its father's name and property by a law which also provides for the care of its mother. This is in marked contrast to the usual treatment of the mother of an illegitimate child, who even when the paternity of her child is acknowledged receives from the father but a pitiful sum for its support; moreover, if the child dies before birth and the mother conceals this fact, although perfectly guiltless of its death, she can be sent to jail for a year.

The age of consent is eighteen years in all of the states in which women have had the ballot, although in only eight of the others is it so high. In the majority of the latter the age of consent is between fourteen and sixteen, and in some of them it is as low as ten. These legal regulations persist in spite of the well-known fact that the mass of girls enter a disreputable life below the age of eighteen. In equal suffrage states important issues regarding women and children, whether of the sweat-shop or the brothel, have always brought out the women voters in great numbers.

Certainly enfranchised women would offer some protection to the white slaves themselves who are tolerated and segregated, but who, because their very existence is illegal, may be arrested whenever any police captain chooses, may be brought before a magistrate, fined and imprisoned. A woman so arrested may be obliged to answer the most harassing questions put to her by a city attorney with no other woman near to protect her from insult. She may be subjected to the most trying examinations in the presence of policemen with no matron to whom to appeal. These things constantly happen everywhere save in Scandinavian countries, where juries of women sit upon such cases and offer the protection of their presence to the prisoners. Without such protection even an innocent woman, made to appear a member of this despised class, receives no consideration. A girl of fifteen recently acting in a South Chicago theatre attracted the attention of a milkman who gradually convinced her that he was respectable. Walking with him one evening to the door of her lodging-house, the girl told him of her difficulties and quite innocently accepted money for the payment of her room rent. The following morning as she was leaving the house the milkman met her at the door and asked her for the five dollars he had given her the night before. When she said she had used it to pay her debt to the landlady, he angrily replied that unless she returned the money at once he would call a policeman and arrest her on a charge of theft. The girl, helpless because she had already disposed of the money, was taken to court, where, frightened and confused, she was unable to give a convincing account of the interview the night before; except for the prompt intervention on the part of a woman, she would either have been obliged to put herself in the power of the milkman, who offered to pay her fine, or she would have been sent to the city prison, not because the proof of her guilt was conclusive, but because her connection with a cheap theatre and the hour of the so-called offence had convinced the court that she belonged to a class of women who are regarded as no longer entitled to legal protection.

Several years ago in Colorado the disreputable women of Denver appealed to a large political club of women against the action of the police who were forcing them to register under the threat of arrest in order later to secure their votes for a corrupt politician. The disreputable women, wishing to conceal their real names and addresses, did not want to be registered, in this respect at least differing from the lodging-house men whose venal votes play such an important part in every municipal election. The women's political club responded to this appeal, and not only stopped the coercion, but finally turned out of office the chief of police responsible for it.

The very fact that the conditions and results of the social evil lie so far away from the knowledge of good women is largely responsible for the secrecy and hypocrisy upon which it thrives. Most good women will probably never consent to break through their ignorance save under a sense of duty which has ever been the incentive to action to which even timid women have responded. At least a promising beginning would be made toward a more effective social control, if the mass of conscientious women were once thoroughly convinced that a knowledge of local vice conditions was a matter of civic obligation, if the entire body of conventional women, simply because they held the franchise, felt constrained to inform themselves concerning the social evil throughout the cities of America. Perhaps the most immediate result would be a change in the attitude toward prostitution on the part of elected officials, responding to that of their constituency. Although good and bad men alike prize chastity in women, and although good men require it of themselves, almost all men are convinced that it is impossible to require it of thousands of their fellow-citizens, and hence connive at the policy of the officials who permit commercialized vice to flourish.

As the first organized Women's Rights movement was inaugurated by the women who were refused seats in the world's Anti-Slavery convention held in London in 1840, although they had been the very pioneers in the organization of the American Abolitionists, so it is quite possible that an equally energetic attempt to abolish white slavery will bring many women into the Equal Suffrage movement, simply because they too will discover that without the use of the ballot they are unable to work effectively for the eradication of a social wrong.

Women are said to have been historically indifferent to social injustices, but it may be possible that, if they once really comprehend the actual position of prostitutes the world over, their sense of justice will at last be freed, and become forevermore a new force in the long struggle for social righteousness. The wind of moral aspiration now dies down and now blows with unexpected force, urging on the movements of social destiny; but never do the sails of the ship of state push forward with such assured progress as when filled by the mighty hopes of a newly enfranchised class. Those already responsible for existing conditions have come to acquiesce in them, and feel obliged to adduce reasons explaining the permanence and so-called necessity of the most evil conditions. On the other hand, the newly enfranchised view existing conditions more critically, more as human beings and less as politicians.

After all, why should the woman voter concur in the assumption that every large city must either set aside well-known districts for the accommodation of prostitution, as Chicago does, or continually permit it to flourish in tenement and apartment houses, as is done in New York? Smaller communities and towns throughout the land are free from at least this semi-legal organization of it, and why should it be accepted as a permanent aspect of city life? The valuable report of the Chicago Vice Commission estimates that twenty thousand of the men daily responsible for this evil in Chicago live outside of the city. They are the men who come from other towns to Chicago in order to see the sights. They are supposedly moral at home, where they are well known and subjected to the constant control of public opinion. The report goes on to state that during conventions or "show" occasions the business of commercialized vice is enormously increased. The village gossip with her vituperative tongue after all performs a valuable function both of castration and retribution; but her fellow-townsman, although grate unconscious of her restraint, coming into a city hotel often experiences a great sense of relief which easily rises to a mood of exhilaration. In addition to this he holds an exaggerated notion of the wickedness of the city. A visiting countryman is often shown museums and questionable sights reserved largely for his patronage, just as tourists are conducted to lurid Parisian revels and indecencies sustained primarily for their horrified contemplation. Such a situation would indicate that, because control is much more difficult in a large city than in a small town, the city deliberately provides for its own inability in this direction.

During a recent military encampment in Chicago large numbers of young girls were attracted to it by that glamour which always surrounds the soldier. On the complaint of several mothers, investigators discovered that the girls were there without the knowledge of their parents, some of them having literally climbed out of windows after their parents had supposed them asleep. A thorough investigation disclosed not only an enormous increase of business in the restricted districts, but the downfall of many young girls who had hitherto been thoroughly respectable and able to resist the ordinary temptations of city life, but who had completely lost their heads over the glitter of a military camp. One young girl was seen by an investigator in the late evening hurrying away from the camp. She was so absorbed in her trouble and so blinded by her tears that she fairly ran against him and he heard her praying, as she frantically clutched the beads around her neck, "Oh, Mother of God, what have I done! What have I done!" The Chicago encampment was finally brought under control through the combined efforts of the park commissioners, the city police, and the military authorities, but not without a certain resentment from the last toward "civilian interference." Such an encampment may be regarded as an historic survival representing the standing armies sustained in Europe since the days of the Roman Empire. These large bodies of men, deprived of domestic life, have always afforded centres in which contempt for the chastity of women has been fostered. The older centres of militarism have established prophylactic measures designed to protect the health of the soldiers, but evince no concern for the fate of the ruined women. It is a matter of recent history that Josephine Butler and the men and women associated with her, subjected themselves to unspeakable insult for eight years before they finally induced the English Parliament to repeal the infamous Contagious Disease Acts relating to the garrison towns of Great Britain, through which the government itself not only permitted vice, but legally provided for it within certain specified limits.

The primary difficulty of military life lies in the withdrawal of large numbers of men from normal family life, and hence from the domestic restraints and social checks which are operative upon the mass of human beings. The great peace propagandas have emphasized the un-justifiable expense involved in the maintenance of the standing armies of Europe, the social waste in the withdrawal of thousands of young men from industrial, commercial and professional pursuits into the barren negative life of the barracks. They might go further and lay stress upon the loss of moral sensibility, the destruction of romantic love, the perversion of the longing for wife and child. The very stability and refinement of the social order depend upon the preservation of these basic emotions.

Social customs are instituted so slowly and even imperceptibly, so far as the conforming individual is concerned, that the mass of men sub-mit to control in spite of themselves, and it is therefore always difficult to determine how far the average upright living is the result of external props, until they are suddenly withdrawn. This is especially true of do-mestic life. Even the sordid marriages in which the senses have forestalled the heart almost always end in some form of family affection. The young couple who may have been brought together in marriage upon the most primitive plane, after twenty years of hard work in meagre, unlovely surroundings, in spite of stupidity and many mistakes, in the face of failure and even wrongdoing, will have unfolded lives of unassuming affection and family devotion to a group of children. They will have faithfully fulfilled that obligation which falls to the lot of the majority of men and women, with its high rewards and painful sacrifices. These rewards as well as the restraints of family life are denied to the soldier. A somewhat similar situation is found in every large construction camp, and in the crowded city tenements occupied by thousands of immigrant men who have preceded their families to America.

In the light of the history of prostitution in relation to militarism, nothing could be more absurd than the familiar statement that virtu-ous women could not safely walk the streets unless opportunity for secret vice were offered to the men of the city. It is precisely the men who have not submitted to self-control who are dangerous and they only, as the court records themselves make clear.

In addition to the large social movements for the betterment of Public Health, for the establishment of Temperance, for the promotion of Equal Suffrage, and for the hastening of Peace and Arbitration is the world-wide organization and active propaganda of International Socialism. It has always included the abolition of this ancient evil in its program of social reconstruction, and since the publication of Bebel's great book, nearly thirty years ago, the leaders of the Socialist party have never ceased to discuss the economics of prostitution with its psychological and moral resultants. The Socialists contend that commercialized vice is fundamentally a question of poverty, a by-product of despair, which will disappear only with the abolition of poverty itself; that it persists not primarily from inherent weakness in human nature, but is a vice arising from a defective organization of social life; that with a reorganization of society, at least all of prostitution which is founded upon the hunger of the victims and upon the profits of the traffickers, will disappear.

Whether we are Socialists or not, we will all admit that every level of culture breeds its own particular brand of vice and uncovers new weaknesses as well as new nobilities in human nature; that a given social development—such, for instance as the conditions of life for thousands of young people in crowded city quarters—may produce such temptations and present such snares to virtue, that average human nature cannot withstand them.

The very fact that the existence of the social evil is semi-legal in large cities is an admission that our individual morality is so uncertain that it breaks down when social control is withdrawn and the opportunity for secrecy is offered. The situation indicates either that the best conscience of the community fails to translate itself into civic action or that our cities are too large to be civilized in a social sense. These difficulties have been enormously augmented during the past century so marked by the rapid growth of cities, because the great principle of liberty has been translated not only into the unlovely doctrine of commercial competition, but also has fostered in many men the belief that personal development necessitates a rebellion against existing social laws. To the opportunity for secrecy which the modern city offers, such men are able to add a high-sounding justification for their immoralities. Fortunately, however, for our moral progress, the specious and illegitimate theories of freedom are constantly being challenged, and a new form of social control is slowly establishing itself on the principle, so widespread in contemporary government, that the state has a responsibility for conditions which determine the health and welfare of its own members;

that it is in the interest of social progress itself that hard-won liberties must be restrained by the demonstrable needs of society.

This new and more vigorous development of social control, while reflecting something of that wholesome fear of public opinion which the intimacies of a small community maintain, is much more closely allied to the old communal restraints and mutual protections to which the human will first yielded. Although this new control is based upon the voluntary co-operation of self-directed individuals, in contrast to the forced submission that characterized the older forms of social restraint, nevertheless in predicting the establishment of adequate social control over the instinct which the modern novelists so often describe as "uncontrollable," there is a certain sanction in this old and well-nigh forgotten history.

The most superficial student of social customs quickly discovers the practically unlimited extent to which public opinion has always regulated marriage. If the traditions of one tribe were endogamous, all the men dutifully married within it; but if the customs of another decreed that wives must be secured by capture or purchase, all the men of that tribe fared forth in order to secure their mates. From the primitive Australian who obtains his wives in exchange for his sisters or daughters, and never dreams of obtaining them in any other way, to the sophisticated young Frenchman, who without objection marries the bride his careful parents select for him; from the ancient Hebrew, who contentedly married the widow of his deceased brother because it was according to the law, to the modern Englishman who refused to marry his deceased wife's sister because the law forbade it, the entire pathway of the so-called uncontrollable instinct has been gradually confined between carefully clipped hedges and has steadily led up to a house of conventional domesticity. Men have fallen in love with their cousins or declined to fall in love with them, very much as custom declared marriages between cousins to be desirable or undesirable, as they formerly married their sisters and later absolutely ceased to desire to marry them. In fact, regulation of this great primitive instinct goes back of the human race itself. All the higher tribes of monkeys are strictly monogamous, and many species of birds are faithful to one mate, season after season. According to the great authority, Forel, prostitution never became established among primitive peoples. Even savage tribes designated the age at which their young men were permitted to assume paternity because feeble children were a drag upon their communal resources. As primitive control lessened with the disappearance of tribal organization and later of the patriarchal family, a social control, not less binding, was slowly established, until throughout the centuries, in spite of many rebellious individuals, the mass of men have lived according to the dictates of the church, the legal requirements of the state, and the surveillance of the community, if only because they feared social ostracism. It is easy, however, to forget these men and their prosaic virtues because history has so long busied herself in recording court amours and the gentle dalliances of the overlord.

The great primitive instinct, so responsive to social control as to be almost an example of social docility, has apparently broken with all the restraints and decencies under two conditions: first and second, when the individual felt that he was above social control and when the individual has had an opportunity to hide his daily living. Prostitution upon a commercial basis in a measure embraces the two conditions, for it becomes possible only in a society so highly complicated that social control may be successfully evaded and the individual thus feels superior to it. When a city is so large that it is extremely difficult to fix individual responsibility, that which for centuries was considered the luxury of the king comes within the reach of every office-boy, and that lack of community control which belonged only to the overlord who felt himself superior to the standards of the people, may be seized upon by any city dweller who can evade his acquaintances. Against such moral aggression, the old types of social control are powerless.

Fortunately, the same crowded city conditions which make moral isolation possible, constantly, tend to develop a new restraint founded upon the mutual dependences of city life and its daily necessities. The city itself socializes the very instruments that constitute the apparatus of social control—Law, Publicity, Literature, Education and Religion. Through their socialization, the desirability of chastity, which has hitherto been a matter of individual opinion and decision, comes to be regarded, not only as a personal virtue indispensable in women and desirable in men, but as a great basic requirement which society has learned to demand because it has been proven necessary for human welfare. To the individual restraints is added the conviction of social responsibility and the whole determination of chastity is reinforced by social sanctions. Such a shifting to social grounds is already obviously taking place in regard to the chastity of women. Formerly all that the best woman possessed was a negative chastity which had been carefully guarded by her parents and duennas. The chastity of the modern woman of self-directed activity and of a varied circle of interests, which gives her an acquaintance with many men as well as women, has therefore a new value and importance in the establishment of social standards. There was a certain basis for the belief that if a woman lost her personal virtue, she lost all; when she had no activity outside of domestic life, the situation itself afforded a foundation for the belief that a man might claim praise for his public career even when his domestic life was corrupt. As woman, however, fulfills her civic obligations while still guarding her chastity, she will be in position as never before to uphold the "single standard," demanding that men shall add the personal virtues to their performance of public duties. Women may at last force men to do away with the traditional use of a public record as a cloak for a wretched private character, because society will never permit a woman to make such excuses for herself.

Every movement therefore which tends to increase woman's share of civic responsibility undoubtedly forecasts the time when a social control will be extended over men, similar to the historic one so long established over women. As that modern relationship between men and women, which the Romans called "virtue between equals" increases, while it will continue to make women freer and nobler, less timid of reputation and more human, will also inevitably modify the standards of men.

On the other hand, there is no doubt that this new freedom from domestic and community control, with the opportunity for escaping observation which the city affords, is often utilized unworthily by women. The report of the Chicago vice commission tells of numerous girls living in small cities and country towns, who come to Chicago from time to time under arrangements made with the landlady of a seemingly respectable apartment. They remain long enough to earn money for a spring or fall wardrobe and return to their home towns, where their acquaintances are quite without suspicion of the methods they have employed to secure the much-admired costumes brought from the city.

Often an unattached country girl, who has come to live in a city, has gradually fallen into a vicious life from sheer lack of social restraint. Such a girl, when living in a smaller community, realized that good behavior was a protective measure and that any suspicion of immorality would quickly ruin her social standing; but when removed from such surveillance, she hopes to be able to pass from her regular life to an irregular one and back again before the fact has been noted, quite as many young men are trying to do.

Perhaps no young woman is more exposed to temptation of this sort than the one who works in an office where she may be the sole woman employed and where the relation to her employer and to her fellow-clerks is almost on a social basis. Many office girls have taken "business courses" in their native towns and have come to the city in search of the large salaries which have no parallels at home. Such a position is not only new to the individual, but it is so recent an outcome of modern business methods, that it has not yet been conventionalized. The girl is without the wholesome social restraint afforded by the companionship of other working-women and her isolation in itself constitutes a danger. An investigation disclosed that a startling number of Chicago girls had found their positions through advertisements and had no means of ascertaining the respectability of their employers. In addition to this, the girls who seek such positions are sometimes vain and pretentious, and will take any sort of office work because it seems to them "more lady-like." A girl of this sort came to Chicago from the country three years ago at the age of seventeen and secured a position as a stenographer with a large firm of lawyers. She was pretty and attractive and in her desire to see more of the wonderful city to which she had come, she accepted many invitations to dinners and theatres from a younger member of the firm. The other girls in the office, representing the more capable type of business women, among whom a careful code of conduct is developing, although at present it is often manifested only by the social ostracism of the one of their number who has broken the conventions, protested against her conduct, first to the girl and then to the head of the office. The usual story developed rapidly, the girl lost her position, her brother-in-law, learning the cause, refused her a home and she became absolutely dependent upon the man. As their relations became notorious, he at length was requested to withdraw from the firm. When brought to my knowledge she had already been deserted for a year. The only people she had known during that time were those in the disreputable hotel in which she had been living when her lover disappeared, and it was through their mistaken kindness in making an opportunity for her in the only life with which they were familiar, that she had been drawn into the worst vice of the city.

She was but one of thousands of young women whose undisciplined minds are fatally assailed by the subtleties and sophistries of city life, and who have lost their bearings in the midst of a multitude of new imaginative impressions. It is hard for a girl, thrilled by the mere propinquity of city excitements and eager to share them, to keep to the gray and monotonous path of regular work. Almost every such girl of the hundreds who have come to grief, "begins" by accepting invitations to dinners and places of amusement. She is always impressed with the ease for concealment which the city affords, although at the same time vaguely resentful that it is so indifferent to her individual existence. It is impossible to estimate the amount of clandestine prostitution which the modern city contains, but there is no doubt that the growth of the social evil at the present moment, lies in this direction. Another of its less sinister developments is perhaps a contemporary manifestation of that break, long considered necessary, between established morality and artistic freedom represented by the hetaira in Athens, the gifted actress in Paris, the geisha in Japan. Insofar as such women have been treated as independent human beings and prized for their mental and social charm, even although they are on a commercial basis, it makes for a humanization of this most sordid business. Such open manifestations of prostitution hasten social control, because publicity has ever been the first step toward community understanding and discipline.

Doubtless the attitude toward the victims of commercialized vice will be modified by many reactions upon the public consciousness, through a thousand manifestations of the great democratic movement which is developing all about us. Certainly we are safe in predicting that when the solidarity of human interest is actually realized, it will become unthinkable that one class of human beings should be sacrificed to the supposed needs of another; when the rights of human life have successfully asserted themselves in contrast to the rights of property, it will become impossible to sell the young and heedless into degradation. An age marked by its vigorous protests against slavery and class tyranny, will not continue to ignore the multitudes of women who are held in literal bondage; nor will an age characterized by a new tenderness for the losers in life's race, always persist in denying forgiveness to the woman who has lost all. A voice which has come across the centuries, filled with pity for her who has "sinned much," must at last be joined by the forgiving voices of others, to whom it has been revealed that it is hardness of heart which has ever thwarted the divine purposes of religion. A generation which has gone through so many successive revolts against commercial aggression and lawlessness, will at last lead one more revolt on behalf of the young girls who are the victims of the basest and vilest commercialism. As that consciousness of human suffering, which already hangs like a black cloud over thousands of our more sensitive contemporaries, increases in poignancy, it must finally include the women who for so many generations have received neither pity nor consideration; as the sense of justice fast widens to encircle all human relations, it must at length reach the women who have so long been judged without a hearing.

In that vast and checkered undertaking of its own moralization to which the human race is committed, it must constantly free itself from the survivals and savage infections of the primitive life from which it started. Now one and then another of the ancient wrongs and uncouth customs which have been so long familiar as to seem inevitable, rise to the moral consciousness of a passing generation; first for uneasy contemplation and then for gallant correction.

May America bear a valiant part in this international crusade of the compassionate, enlisting under its banner not only those sensitive to the wrongs of others, but those conscious of the destruction of the race itself, who form the standing army of humanity's self-pity, which is becoming slowly mobilized for a new conquest!

Index

Abbott, Grace, xviii
abolition movement, 3–6, 90
accidents, industrial-related, 35
action: absence of, 45; emotions as precursor to, 7; examples of, 48; social movements linked to, 82–83
Adams, George Matthew, xxviii
Addams, Jane: literary negotiations by, xviii–xx; milieu of, ix–x; as pragmatist and intellectual, xxii–xxiii; reasons for going to Chicago, x; response to writing of, xxvii–xxviii; stories told by, xvi–xvii, xx–xxi; works: *Democracy and Social Ethics*, xix; *A New Conscience and an Ancient Evil*, x, xviii, xx–xxiii, xxvii–xxix; *Newer Ideals of Peace*, xix; *The Spirit of Youth and the City Streets*, xix; *Twenty Years at Hull-House*, x, xvii, xix
advertisements (newspaper), 40–41
African Americans: as domestic workers, 77; housing for, 55
alcohol: access to, 15; effects of, 69–71; social movement against, 85–87; as temptation, 52–53; wages spent on, 75. *See also* saloons
Alice of Windsor (princess), x
Alliance for the Suppression and Prevention of the White Slave Traffic, 5
American Purity Federation, 5

Armstrong, Eliza, xii
athletics, as counter to temptations, 49
"The Awakening of Spring" (Wedekind), 46

Bakhtin, Mikhail, xvi
Balzac, Honoré de, xii–xiii
Bebel (writer), 93
Behrend, B. H., xxix
Billington-Grieg, Teresa, xiii
Bingham (police commissioner), 87
birth control, social effects of, xii
Booth, Charles, 39
Bowen, Joseph Tilton, xxvi
Bowen, Louise de Koven, xxvi
boys: prosecutions against, 24; protective legislation for, 58–59; sex education for, 47; temptations for, 49–50, 58–59
Brett, George P.: on Addams's writing, xvii, xxvii, xxviii; negotiations with, xviii–xix
Butler, Josephine, xii, 91

cadet: presence of, xxi–xxii; use of term, xxvii–xxviii. *See also* pandering
Campbell, Helen, xxiv
Catholicism, 48
chastity: as basic requirement, 95–96; context for maintaining, 27; men's

support for, 89; type of girls who lose, 50–51, 52, 63

Chicago: alcohol sales in, 85–86; appeal of, ix, xi; children's protective legislation in, 58–59, 62–63; entertainment venues in, 70–72; exposé of, xii; ill children in, 84; juvenile courts in, 50–51, 55–56, 57, 79; military camp in, 91; prostitution districts in, 90–91; prostitution profits in, 27–28; saloons in, 52; sex education in, 45–46; street solicitation in, 23–24; white slave traffic confronted by, 12; women's social/cultural role in, xi. *See also* Juvenile Protective Association of Chicago; Vice Commission of Chicago

Chicago Municipal Court, 14

child labor movement, 62

children and youth: diseases of, 83–84; illegitimate (in Norway), 87; imaginations of, 49–50; mother's giving up, 78–79; non-moral type of, 56–57; protective legislation for, 57–59, 62–63; public concern and support for, 54–55, 60–62; sex education for, 45–49; temptations faced by, 51–60. *See also* boys; girls

clothing: desire for stylish, 39, 96–97; lack of spending on, 74, 75

Colorado, women voters in, 89

colored. *See* African Americans

Columbus, regulating entertainment venues in, 71

Connelly, Mark, xxx–xxxi n. 15

conscience: analogy for, 3–8; difficulties faced by, 93–94; emergence of, 45–46; philanthropy as evidence of, 64

consumers, as influence, 42–43

Contagious Disease Acts (England), 91

crime commissions. *See* vice and crime commissions

dance halls, 49–50, 69, 86

Davis, Allen, xvii, xxiii

Dedrick, Florence Mabel, ix, x–xi, xxiii

degeneracy, use of term, 11

delivery/messenger boys, temptations for, 58–59

demoralization, 11, 68, 79

Denver, women voters in, 89

department stores, rest rooms in, 40–41

department store workers: difficulties faced by, 30–31; education of, 60; parental control of, 74–75; wages of, 29–30, 32

dependents, economic responsibility for, 28–30, 32–33. *See also* families

deportation, as threat, 17

Dewey, John, xxii

diseases: exposure to vice and, 57; industrial-related, 34–35; social evil linked to, 60–62, 82–85

domestic workers: dangers faced by, 35, 55, 66, 72–73, 76–78; as prostitutes, 43, 73–74, 76, 79–80, 80; suicides of, 78–79; taken in white slave trade, 9–10

Doubleday, Frank, xvii

Dreiser, Theodore: as possible model, xxv; sisters of, xiii; works: *Jennie Gerhardt*, xx, xxvi–xxvii; *Sister Carrie*, xiv

economic conditions: department store workers and, 29–31; dependents as factor in, 28–30, 32–33; exposure to vice and, 52–53, 93; means for improving, 42–44; mental health linked to, 16, 37–38; for out-of-work girls, 40–41; reports and statistics on, 26–28; upswing in prostitution as reflection of, 36–37. *See also* prostitution, economics of

education: about diseases, 84; about sexuality, 45–49; in healthful play, 51–52; responsibilities of, 57–58, 59; as social control mechanism, 95–96; of workers, 60

Ellis Island, 13, 73

Elshtain, Jean Bethke, xxii

emotions: abuse of, 16–17, 37; in response to white slave trade, 6–8 entertainment and leisure: dangers in, 32; recruiting girls in venues of, 68–72; sexual slant of, 15; streets' role in, 38–39; temptations in, 51–52, 98. *See also* athletics, as counter to temptations; dance halls; theatres

eugenics, 60–61

Ewen, Elizabeth, xxvi

excursion boats, recruiting girls on, 71

factory workers: difficulties faced by, 34–35; downtown workers compared to, 33–34; education of, 60; social spaces for, 38–39; wages of, 35–36, 37–38

families: affection's growth in, 92; living and social spaces of, 38–40; out-of-work daughters and, 40–41; parental tyranny in, 73–76; sex education and, 45–46; wages sent to, 67, 72. *See also* children and youth; dependents; marriage

Federation of Woman's Clubs, xxiii

Fields, James T., xvii

Forel (writer), 94

friendships, need for, 80–81

garment workers: difficulties faced by, 15–16, 23, 40; trade unionism and, 38; wages of, 74

Germany, sex education in, 46

Gerusalem, Elsa, 7

Gilman, Charlotte Perkins, xiii, xxiii, xxiv–xxv

girls: childbearing of, 78–79, 81; from country, 66–68, 96–97; cynicism of, 74; education of, 60; military as alluring to, 91–92; obedience of, 73–74; recruitment of, 68–72; rescue of, 62–63, 65–66; temptations for, 51–53; type in prostitution, 50–51, 52, 56–57, 59, 63, 64–65. *See also* working girls

Goethe, Johann Wolfgang von, 51

Goldman, Emma, xiii

gossip, function of, xxv, 90–91. *See also* public opinion

Great Britain: children's protective legislation in, 59, 62; Minimum Wage Boards in, 38; prostitution in, xii, 54, 91; sex education in, 46, 47; unemployment in, 60

Hamilton, Alice, xx

Harper's (magazine), xxviii

Harper's (publisher), xiv

health: commitment to public, 84–85; domestic's loss of, 77–78; social movement and, 82–84. *See also* diseases; mental health

Herbst, H. H., xxviii–xxix

Hobson, Barbara Meil, xiii

Holmes, Oliver Wendell, xxii

Houghton, Henry, xvii

hours: legislation on, 34–35, 72; of working girls, 27–29, 32, 37–38, 42–43

housing, search for affordable, 53–55

Howell-Bennett Act (1907), 13

Hull-House settlement: as center of academic activity, xxii; day nursery at, 53–54; founding of, x; Gilman's stay at, xxiii–xxiv; girls assisted at, 19

human nature: companionship needs in, 16–17; friendship needs in, 80–81; weaknesses in, 65, 93

human progress: components of, 7; social movements for, 82–83; solidarity in, 98–99

Huron Valley Building and Savings Association, xxviii

Illinois: pandering law in, 12; protective legislation in, 58, 72; public support for children in, 54

imagination: perverted by temptations, 51–59, 77, 98; self-control of, 49–50

immigrant girls: in juvenile court, 50–51; obedience of, 73–74; temptations and dangers for, 13–17, 72–73; wages of, 37–38

immigrants: protection needed by, 17–18; white slave traffic linked to, 13–15

Immigrants' Protective League, 14, 37
immigration laws, 12, 17–18
Industrial Commission of Wisconsin, 38
industrialism: accidents/diseases and,
34–35; investigation of, 42–44. *See also*
factory workers
Institute of Electrical Engineers, xxix
International Agreement for the Suppression of the White Slave Traffic, xii

James, William, xxii
Jorgan, Elizabeth G., xxviii
Joseph T. Bowen Country Club, xxvi
Juvenile Protective Association of Chicago: investigations and arrests by, 41,
57; report by, xv, xvii, xxv, 1–2, 66;
saloon closure and, 52; women and
girls rescued by, xxi, 16, 66–81

Kansas City: lodging houses in, 42; regu-
lating entertainment venues in, 71
Kelley, Florence, xx
Kelly, Howard, 63
Kneeland, George, xii

Lansey, Charlotte Howett, xxvii
Lasch, Christopher, xxii
laundry workers, difficulties faced by,
35, 72
laws: on age of consent, 87–88; children's protective, 57–59, 62–63; on
hours, 34–35, 72; immigration, 12, 17–
18; international cases and, 9–12; possible changes in, 6, 42; prostitutes as
outside of, 65; prostitution as semi-
legal in, 93–94; as social control
mechanism, 95–96; state cases and,
13–14; on street solicitation, 23–24
League of Cook County Clubs, 63
Lecky (writer), 3
leisure. *See* entertainment and leisure
Lincoln, Abraham, 6
Lippmann, Walter, xxiii
literature: shortcomings of youth, 49; as
social control mechanism, 95–96;
understanding gained via, 7–8

lodging houses: investigation of, 42;
raids of, 69–70
Lyttleton (schoolmaster), 47

Macmillan (publisher), xvii–xx, xxiii,
xxvii, xxviii
magic, beliefs in, 56
Mann Act (1910), xii
marriage: Addams's emphasis on, xxii,
xxv, 28, 67; affection's growth in, 92;
custom's regulation of, 94–95; opportunities for, 76; as ploy, 14, 17, 19–20;
postponement of, 30; prostitution
compared to, xiii, xxiv; prostitution
continued in, 10–11, 24–25
Marsh, Edward, xvii, xix–xx
Massachusetts: crime commission in,
xiii, xv; minimum wage study in, 38
McClure, Samuel S. (*McClure's Magazine*), xviii–xx, xxiii, xxvii, 1
Melville, Herman, ix
men: marriage postponed by, 30; prostitutes used by, 90–91; social control of,
96–97; in standing armies, 91–92;
wife/prostitute and, 24–25
Menand, Louis, xxii
mental health: exposure to vice and, 55–
56, 57; of immigrants, 16, 37–38; of
out-of-work girls, 41–42. *See also*
health
middle class: attitudes toward domestic
workers, 77–79; as audience for narratives, xv, xxix, 7–8, 98–99; commercialized vice contemplated by, 6–7;
poor women as threat to, xvi; prostitutes as distressing to, 64–65; sense of
duty of, 89
military, social evil linked to, 91–92
Milwaukee, regulating entertainment
venues in, 71
Minnesota, vice commission in, 5
Moody Church (Chicago), ix
morality: in abolition movement, 3–4;
artistic freedom and, 98; breakdown
of, 93–94; of domestic workers, 80; of
factory workers, 33–34; lack of devel-

opment of, 14, 56–57; as ruse in accusations, 20–21; wages linked to, 32, 36–37. *See also* demoralization

moral panic: about prostitution, xii–xiii; about women's move to city, xv–xvi

More, Sir Thomas, 62

National Society for the Scientific Study of Education, 46

National Vigilance Committee, 5

newsboys, temptations for, 58–59

New York, children's protective legislation in, 58

New York City, regulating entertainment venues in, 71

New York Night Court, 22–23

New York Society for the Prevention of Cruelty to Children, 51

Norway, illegitimate children in, 87

obedience, of domestic workers, 73–74

occupations, limits on children's, 58. *See also* working girls; *specific occupations*

office workers, difficulties faced by, 97–98

Ohio, regulating entertainment venues in, 71

Oregon, ten-hour law in, 34–35

Page, Walter Hines, xvii

palmists, vice linked to, 56

pandering: law against, 12; recruiting tactics in, 69–72; training for, 50. *See also* cadet

parks, recreational opportunities in, 71

Peirce, Charles Sanders, xxii

Peiss, Kathy, xi–xii

philanthropic organizations: abolition as goal of, 65–66, 98–99; children's diseases and, 84; dangerous public spaces and, 68; friendship as force for, 81; lack of efforts in, 64–65; recreation recommended by, 71–72. *See also* Hull-House settlement; Juvenile Protective Association of Chicago

Phillips, David Graham, xiv

Plato, 62

police and police departments: corruption of, 18–20, 22; lodging house raided by, 69–70; prostitutes questioned/harassed by, 88; prostitutes registered with, 59, 89; reprimands for, 20–22

politicians and politics: corruption of, 18–19, 21–22, 89; saloon protected by, 52

poor and poor working women: assumptions about, xxii; children's exposure to vice and, 52–53; difficulties faced by, xvi; sexual behavior of, xxv; as socially marginal/symbolically central, xv–xvi; social worker's distance from, xxiii. *See also* housing; stories; working girls

pragmatism, xiv, xxii–xxiii

preventive associations, 4

prison, avoidance of, 67–68

prostitution: absent in primitive societies, 94–95; acceptance of, 19–20, 65, 89, 90–91; African Americans in, 55; alcohol's role in, 85–87; approaches to, 4–6; corruption linked to, 3–4, 18–19; definitions of, xi–xii; department store workers in, 29–30, 32, 75; domestic workers in, 43, 73–74, 76, 79–80; economics of, xiii–xiv, 4, 10–11, 36–37, 93; factory workers in, 35–36, 39; garment worker in, 40; international differences in treatment of, 23–24; motivation in, 22, 28–29; narratives of, xv–xvii, xxv, xxx–xxxi n. 15; new conscience about, 3–8; obsession with, ix–x; office worker in, 98; panic about, xii–xiii; paradox of, 11; regulation vs. illegality of, 18–19; semi-legal status of, 93–94; vulnerability to, xiv–xv; wages for, 27–28, 32; waitresses in, 32–33; young girls in, 50–51, 56–57, 59, 64–65. *See also* social evil; vice and crime commissions; white slave trade

public: education of, 84; pharisaic attitude of, 18–19. *See also* social class

public opinion: breakdown of influence by, 48–49, 80; fear of, 94; function of,

90–91; as social control mechanism, 94–96

public space: dangers inherent in, 68–70; leisure activities in, xi–xii, 49–50. *See also* streets

publishing, expansion of, xvii–xviii

purity leagues, xiv

Putnam, George Palmer, xvii

Rabelais, François, xiii

race, sexuality linked to, xi. *See also* African Americans

racism, in sex trade discourse, xiv

reform efforts: as analogy for new conscience, 3–8; for children's protective legislation, 57–59, 62–63. *See also* philanthropic organizations

religion: sexual disease and, 84; as social control mechanism, 95–96; youth activities and, 47–48

rescue homes: friendships in, 81; girls in, 35, 40, 62–63; interviews of women in, 29; underground railroad compared to, 4

restaurants, alcohol in, 69–70. *See also* saloons

Roe, Clifford G.: cases prosecuted by, 12, 19, 24; on girls from country, 66; on sex trade, ix, xxv

Rosen, Ruth, xiii, xiv

Rosenwald, Julius, xxvi

saloons: alcohol sales in, 86; country girls arrested in, 67–68; dance halls connected to, 69, 86; temptations of, 52–53

Salvation Army, 81

sanitary science, development of, 84–85

Sawyer, Charles N., xxviii

Scribner, Charles, xvii

self-confidence, as danger, xxi–xxii

self-control, lessons in, 48–49

settlement movement, xxiv. *See also* Hull-House settlement

sex trade. *See* prostitution; social evil; white slave trade

sexuality: avoiding hint of, xxiii; commodification of, xxv; public spaces and, xi–xii, 49–50; teaching about, 45–49

Seymour, Ralph Fletcher, xxviii

Shaw, Bernard, 7

Sims, Edwin W., ix, 11–12, 22

slavery, as analogy to prostitution, 3–6

slum angels, Addams's concept of, xxi–xxii

small-pox epidemic, sexual disease compared to, 83

Smith, Mary Rozet, xx

social change: dis-ease with, xxvi–xxvii; modern urban woman's role in, xxii–xxiii; sexuality's role in, 46–47; socially marginal/symbolically central issue in, xv–xvi

social class: assumptions based in, xxii; prostitution and, xiii; sexuality linked to, xi. *See also* middle class; poor and poor working women

social control: freedom from, xvi, 14–15, 26, 75–76, 93–94; increased need for, 93–96; of military, 91–92; of office workers, 97–98; prostitution districts and, 90–91. *See also* social movements

social evil: abolition of, 5, 42–44, 65–66, 83–84, 98–99; alcohol's role in, 85–87; cities' differing approaches to, 17–19; definition of, 6; diseases linked to, 60–62, 82–85; equal suffrage as counter to, 87–91; lack of philanthropic effort to confront, 64–65; literary treatment of, 7–8; military linked to, 91–92; resource to combat, 6–7; social control's role in, 93–96; Socialism as counter to, 92–93; suggested legalization of, 63. *See also* prostitution; white slave trade

Socialism, social movement for, 92–93

social justice: as appeal, 65–66; developing recognition of, 89–90

social movements: against alcohol, 85–87; censorship by (purity), xii–xiii; against diseases, 82–85; for equal suf-

frage, 87–91; for International Socialism, 92–93
social work, writing about vs. doing,
xxiv. *See also* Hull-House settlement
Stallybrass, Peter, xv
Stange, Margit, xxiii
Starr, Ellen Gates, x
Stead, William, xii
stories: Addams's use of, xvi–xvii, xx–
xxi, xxv; of country girls who came to
city, 66–68, 96–97; of French girl
(Marie), xxi, 9–12; of immigrant girl's
rescue (Olga), xxi, 15–17; of man's
wife/prostitute, 24–25; of Norwegian
domestic worker, 77–78; of office
workers, 97–98; of parental control,
73–76; of recruiting girls in entertainment venues, 69–72; of suicides and
attempted suicides, 39–40, 78–79. *See
also* working girls
streets: as social space, 38–39; suppress-
ing solicitation in, 23–24. *See also*
public space
Sudermann (writer), 7
suffrage: as counter to social evil, 87–91;
for freedmen, 4
sympathetic understanding concept, 7–8

Tebbel, John, xvii
theatres: allure of, 9–10, 49; attitudes
toward, 88; girls recruited at, 70–71;
prostitution linked to, 21–22, 52
Tolstoy, Leo, 81
trade unionism, 38, 42

underground railroad, 4
unemployed workers: difficulties faced
by, 40–42, 59; types of, 60
U.S. Congress, on white slave trade, 12
U.S. Supreme Court, on ten-hour law,
34–35
urban areas: African American gender
imbalance in, 77; children's protective
legislation in, 58–59; civic responsibilities in, 96–97; differing approaches
of, 17–19; girls from country in, 66–68,

96–97; as locus of white slave trade,
13; milk supply in, 61; moral panic
about women's move to, xv–xvi; public health concerns in, 84–85; regulating entertainment venues in, 71; self-
control absent in, 48–49; single,
out-of-work girls in, 41–42; social
control needed in, 93–96. *See also*
entertainment and leisure; public
space; streets
Utah, diseases reported in, 85

vice: effects of exposure to, 52–53, 55–56,
57, 93; legal control of, 22–23; starvation vs., 23–24
vice and crime commissions: difficulties
ahead for, 5–6; on female sexual vulnerability, xiv; on prostitution, xi–xii,
xiii, xiv–xv
Vice Commission of Chicago: on alcohol sales, 86; on child workers, 58; on
country girls, 96–97; on female sexual
vulnerability, xiv; on male customers,
90–91; on police corruption, 18; on
prostitution and wages, 27–28; prostitution's abolishment supported by, 5
Vice Commission of Minneapolis, 5
virtue, cynicism about, 74
vocational bureaus, 42, 59

wages: levels of, 60; parental expectations of, 38, 73–76; sent to distant
families, 67, 72; of working girls, 27–
30, 32, 35–36, 37–38, 42–43
waitresses, difficulties faced by, 32–33
Wald, Lillian, xviii, xx
Walkowitz, Judith, xii
Wedekind (writer), 46
Weeks, Jeffrey, xv
Wells (writer), 53
White, Allon, xv
White, Stanford, xxix
white slave trade: cities' differing approaches to, 17–19; concerns about, 1–
2; country girls for, 66–68, 96–97;
emotional response to knowledge of,

6–7; exposé on, ix; extreme youth in, 56–58; getting out of, xiv; Gilman on, xxiv–xxv; governmental investigations of, 43–44; international regulations and treaty on, 3–4, 12; international traffic in, 9–15; interstate cases of, 19–20; as myth, x, xiii; narratives of, xv–xvii, xxx–xxxi n. 15; obsession with, ix–x; panic about, xii–xiii; pity and, 62; resistance to, 15–17; rest rooms as places for procuring girls for, 40–41; supply of women for, 26, 28–29, 79–80; use of term, xiv. *See also* prostitution; social evil; vice and crime commissions
White Slave Traffic Act (1910), 12, 22
White Slave Traffic Committee, 62–63
Willets, Phoebe, xxvii
Wisconsin: children's protective legislation in, 58; minimum wage study in, 38; regulating entertainment venues in, 71

women. *See* poor and poor working women; prostitution; working girls
"Women and Child Wage Earners in the United States" (report), 32, 38, 76
women's organizations: children's protective legislation sought by, 62–63; sex education by, 45–47
Women's Wear (magazine), xxviii
working girls: as factory workers, 33–39, 60; improving conditions for, 42–44; in laundries, 35, 72; number of, 26–27; in offices, 97–98; social spaces for, 38–39, 42; temptations for, 69–71; unemployment and, 40–42, 59, 60; as waitresses, 32–33. *See also* department store workers; domestic workers; hours; immigrant girls; stories; wages
workplace, dangers facing immigrant girls in, 14–15, 72–73
World War I, opposition to, xxviii

Zola, Émile, xiii

JANE ADDAMS (1860–1935) was a social activist, a leading Progressive reformer, public speaker, author of many books of social criticism, and an original theorist who contributed to the development of American sociology and pragmatist philosophy. Her feminism, pacifism, and pragmatist experimentalism found concrete expression in the institutions she founded or to which she gave early support, including the Hull-House settlement in Chicago, the National Association for the Advancement of Colored People, the National American Woman Suffrage Association, the American Civil Liberties Union, and the Woman's International League for Peace and Freedom. She was awarded the Nobel Peace Prize in 1931.

KATHERINE JOSLIN is the author of *Edith Wharton* and coeditor of *Wretched Exotic: Essays on Edith Warton in Europe*. Her scholarly work includes essays on Jane Addams, Willa Cather, Kate Chopin, Theodore Dreiser, George Sand, Virginia Woolf, and Émile Zola. A professor of English at Western Michigan University, Joslin directs an interdisciplinary program in American studies and has conducted Fulbright Summer Institutes in the Study of the United States for International Professors. The WMU Alumni Association awarded her its Teaching Excellence Award in 1997.

The University of Illinois Press
is a founding member of the
Association of American University Presses.

Composed in 10.5/13 Minion
with Nueva Bold display
by Celia Shapland
for the University of Illinois Press
Manufactured by Thomson-Shore, Inc.

University of Illinois Press
1325 South Oak Street
Champaign, IL 61820-6903
www.press.uillinois.edu